150 FAQs About
Revelation
and the End
of the World

By Samuel F. Parvin
and C. Stephen Byrum

Abingdon Press
Nashville

UNLOCKING THE MYSTERIES:
150 FAQS ABOUT REVELATION AND THE END OF THE WORLD

Copyright © 1999 by Abingdon Press

This book is printed on recycled, acid-free paper.

Cover design by Shawn Marie Lancaster
Cover illustration by Angus McBride/Linden Artists

99 00 01 02 03 04 05 06 07 08 —10 9 8 7 6 5 4 3 2 1

MANUFACTURED IN THE UNITED STATES OF AMERICA

Contents

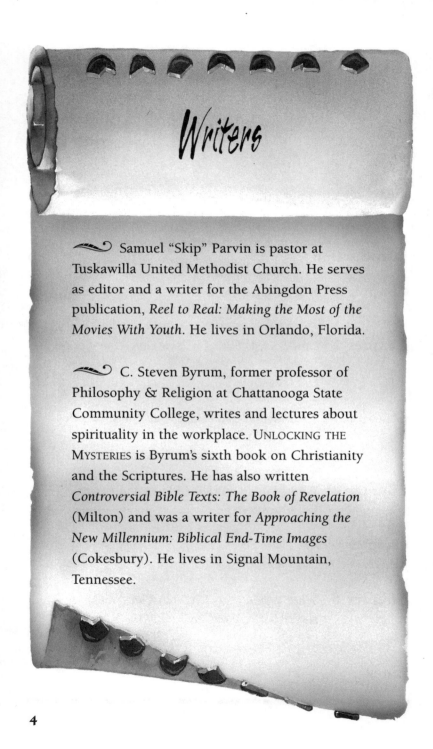

Writers

Samuel "Skip" Parvin is pastor at Tuskawilla United Methodist Church. He serves as editor and a writer for the Abingdon Press publication, *Reel to Real: Making the Most of the Movies With Youth*. He lives in Orlando, Florida.

C. Steven Byrum, former professor of Philosophy & Religion at Chattanooga State Community College, writes and lectures about spirituality in the workplace. UNLOCKING THE MYSTERIES is Byrum's sixth book on Christianity and the Scriptures. He has also written *Controversial Bible Texts: The Book of Revelation* (Milton) and was a writer for *Approaching the New Millennium: Biblical End-Time Images* (Cokesbury). He lives in Signal Mountain, Tennessee.

Introduction

Why another book about Revelation?

I magine a time filled with interpretations of when and how the world will end. Visions of mass destruction at the end of time are commonplace. Most of these interpreters attempt to tie current events to the images and symbols found in the Book of Revelation. Reports of bizarre creatures and outrageous events are everywhere. People are convinced that Jesus is coming in the clouds at any moment. A deadly disease for which there seems to be no cure ravages human beings. The world is torn apart by wars and terrorism. There are famines, earthquakes, floods, and fires, all seen as signs that the end of the world is near. There is a blatant disregard for the poor. Crime and carnage are everywhere. No one feels he or she can trust the persons who have been chosen to lead them because of the corruption and lack of integrity in high office. World leaders attempt to undermine one another, and some even think it might be to their advantage to have rival leaders assassinated. The Middle East is the source of great political strife, and extremists attempt to be heard through violent acts that injure innocent people.

Sound like the world we live in just before the turn of the twenty -first century? Surprise! This is a description of the world in A.D. 999, just before the year 1000. The world went crazy before the year 1000 in much the same way it seems to be going crazy around the year 2000. Many people were certain that the world would end in the year 1000 and attempted to justify their predictions by pointing to the Book of Revelation.

As we begin the third millennium, Christians need to understand more than ever what the Book of Revelation has to say about the times in which we live.

How is this book, UNLOCKING THE MYSTERIES, different from other books about Revelation?

*M*any other books focus on the sensational aspects of the Book of Revelation. Gloom and doom take center stage, and the emphasis is on the disturbing and frightening aspects of the last book of the Bible. There is no doubt that the Book of Revelation deals with the end of the world. There is also no doubt that the Book of Revelation talks about judgment. But if we focus only on the disturbing parts, we will miss the most important point that Revelation makes: This is a book about being Christian during times and circumstances when it is hard to be a Christian.

The Christians of John's time were threatened with prison, persecution, and even death for believing in Jesus Christ. But John believed his vision would give these persecuted Christians courage and hope to face the future unafraid, resting in the knowledge that a good and loving God was in control of creation even when it seemed like God wasn't there at all. The people of John's time needed to be encouraged to stand firm in their faith and to continue to live their lives in Christian love, knowing that evil could never finally win because God was with them every step of the way.

UNLOCKING THE MYSTERIES not only looks at what Revelation has to say about the end of the world, but also at what Jesus had to say about it. Many people don't realize that Jesus taught his disciples a great deal about the end of time. When combined with the Book of Revelation, Jesus' teachings about the end of time spoke a message of undying hope to those first-century Christians, just as it speaks the same message of eternal hope to us.

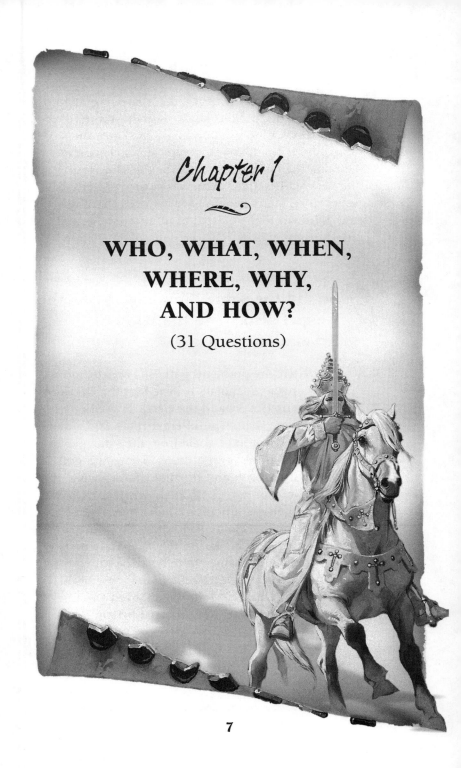

Chapter 1

WHO, WHAT, WHEN, WHERE, WHY, AND HOW?

(31 Questions)

1 Who wrote the Book of Revelation?

Across the centuries, there have been countless discussions about who the author of the Book of Revelation might be. Since the name John is used, the most typical conclusion has been that the book was written by the same John, "the Beloved Disciple," who was at the core of the gospel story. Many people have believed that this same John wrote the Gospel of John; First, Second, and Third John; as well as the Book of Revelation.

2 So did the same John who wrote the Gospel also write the Book of Revelation?

There are problems with this conclusion. Language scholars believe that the Greek of John's Gospel and the Greek of the Book of Revelation were written at different times and almost certainly could not have come from the same person. In all likelihood, the John of Jesus' day would not have lived until the end of the first century when the Book of Revelation was most likely written. Of course, it would be difficult to find a much more common name than John; so to draw the conclusion that all of the "John books" in the New Testament were written by the same "John" may be unreasonable. But there is still disagreement among biblical scholars about whether "John the Beloved Disciple" and "John the Revealer" are the same person.

3 Who was John the Revealer?

It is probable that a certain John functioned in a bishop-like role over a section of Asia Minor where the seven churches mentioned early in Revelation were located. It makes sense that a church leader would have written these words to influence and help the churches under his responsibility during times of persecution. But no one knows for sure.

4 Where was the Book of Revelation written?

John tells us he had his vision while exiled on the island of Patmos. Patmos sits about forty miles off the southwest coast of present-day Turkey, not far from the famed ancient city of Miletus.

5 Why was John exiled to Patmos?

Most traditions report that Patmos was a place of exile for those who opposed the Roman Empire; it was a place where dissidents were sent to be punished with a life of hard labor rather than being put to death. According to tradition, John the Revealer was exiled there by the Emperor Domitian in A.D. 95 for eighteen months; and it was during this time that he received the vision that led to the Book of Revelation. The Bible is not totally clear about why John was sent there. Revelation 1:9 does indicate that John was at Patmos "on account of the word of God and the testimony of

Jesus." The fact that he was exiled to Patmos supports the idea that John the Revealer was a significant leader of the Christian church in that region.

6 Why did John write Revelation?

In the very first verse, John tells us that God sent an angel to show him a vision of the events that would happen. John's experience was not very different from those of some other people in the Bible. God spoke to Ezekiel through a vision of dry bones that came to life (Ezekiel 37:1-14). Daniel received a vision from God that allowed him to interpret a dream for the king and save many lives (Daniel 2:19-49). God sent Peter a vision that directed him to preach to the Gentiles (Acts 10:9-33). Paul's vision on the Damascus Road changed his life (Acts 9:3-8). John says he was "in the spirit on the Lord's Day," when he heard a loud voice behind him directing him to "write in a book what you see and send it to the seven churches" (Revelation 1:10-11).

7 When was the Book of Revelation written?

The New Testament period can be divided into four general time frames to provide key reference points:

(1) A.D. 1–50: Jesus lived during this period; and following his death and resurrection, the early church formed. Little material about the life, death, and resurrection of Jesus was actually

written down, probably because attention was given to the work at hand; and because after Jesus ascended into heaven, it was popularly believed that Jesus would return at any time.

(2) A.D. 50–75: During this period, the writings of Paul and the first Gospel accounts become available, telling the story of Jesus and the early church to new generations and attempting to give guidance to the churches that were being established. From A.D. 64–66 the first persecutions of Christians took place under Nero.

(3) A.D. 75–90: During this period, the Christian church began to spread throughout the Roman Empire.

(4) A.D. 90–100: This decade marks a significant crisis of faith and a time of greatest vulnerability for the early Christian community. It was during this period that the church experienced heightened persecution by its enemies, especially during the rule of the emperor Domitian.

The Book of Revelation was most likely written during the fourth time frame (A.D. 90–100). Its symbols and images fit well with the events and personalities that rose to importance at the end of the first century. Its meanings and messages would have given great comfort to Christians experiencing persecution then. The book makes the most sense when it is seen in light of what was happening to the Christian community during this time. These factors would date the Book of Revelation somewhere between A.D. 90 and 100. The Greek used in the book also matches well with the way the Greek language was written at that time.

8 *Q* What do the words *revelation* and *apocalypse* mean?

A In our time these words evoke feelings and images of danger, evil, and the mysterious. Those feelings and images may have been what the writer of Revelation wanted his readers to experience also.

The earlier of these two words, *apocalypse*, literally means "hidden realities, which are now unveiled." That does sound a bit eerie and frightening! People who believed strongly in apocalyptic ideas felt that there were at least two levels to life—an obvious, surface level that we encounter in day-to-day existence, and a concealed, beneath-the-surface level that most people would not notice. This second level was the hidden, which was in need of being unveiled. *Revelation* is a word that suggests the unveiling of those hidden ideas.

9 *Q* Why are there so many weird creatures, symbols, people, and places?

A Apocalyptic writings emerge in times of great trial and crisis. This type of literature has a particular way of looking at the world and God's role in it. It sees time divided into two ages: the present, which is evil, and the time to come, a time of peace. In the present are images of cosmic battle between good and evil, of upheaval, of great distress. But the underlying message is to hang on, because ultimately God will triumph! The weird and puzzling images are symbolic, a bit like a code. Some people would "get it"; others would not.

10 Why would John want to write this way?

Fantastic images, cosmic clashes, and mystery intrigue many people. Even today there are large audiences for science-fiction books and movies, horror stories, and the mysterious. John wanted both to attract readers and to give them a message with far deeper meaning than just good, scary writing. Also, he needed to write in such a way as to deliver the message to the believers (and potential believers) without the persecutors becoming wise to it. It was not safe to speak out.

11 Are there other apocalyptic writings in the Bible?

Yes. In the Old Testament, Daniel (Chapters 2 and 7–12); Ezekiel 1; Isaiah 24–27; and Zechariah 12–14 are examples of this type of writing. In the New Testament, portions of two letters by Paul use that style: 1 Thessalonians 4:13-18 and 2 Thessalonians 2:1-12. The Gospels describe Jesus himself as talking in apocalyptic terms about the destruction of Jerusalem and the end of the age (Mark 13; Matthew 24; Luke 17:22-37; 21:5-36).

12 Q Does the Bible have other special kinds of writing?

A Yes. The Bible is made up of many different types of writing: history (like First and Second Samuel); narratives (like Acts); law (like Leviticus); Gospels (Matthew, Mark, Luke, and John); wisdom (like Proverbs); poetry (like the Psalms); and letters (like Paul's letter to the Romans). The Bible is really like a library of many types of religious writings.

Different types of writing fulfill different needs and different purposes. For instance, a recipe book provides instructions for preparing food. A diary fulfills the need for people to record their thoughts and the things that happen to them. A novel is written to entertain us. This idea that the way something is written depends on who it is being written for and what its purpose is also applies to the different kinds of writing we find in the Bible. For example, a book of history fulfills the need of making people aware of their roots. A book of law gives people a basic set of moral principles by which to live. A Gospel tells them about the life and teachings of Jesus. Again, the key point is that different types of books in the Bible fulfill different needs.

13 Q What special needs does Revelation fulfill?

A The apocalyptic writing in Revelation fulfills a unique set of needs. By its nature, it gets people's attention. It may—by design—even scare people into listening to what it has to say.

But John also wanted the Book of Revelation to give Christians hope as they lived in those terribly desperate times. The church was undergoing tremendous persecution. Many Christians were giving in to fear and leaving the church. It was also a time when converting to Christianity would have had very little appeal. The church's whole future might have been jeopardized. So John told the story of his vision in a way that would speak to these many needs.

14 How did the message of Revelation help give these persecuted Christians courage and hope?

Remember that at the end of the first century the Christian church in Asia Minor (where the author of the Book of Revelation most likely lived) was severely persecuted by outside enemies, and it was difficult to keep a high level of commitment among the faithful, much less bring new people into the church. So the message of Revelation served two very important purposes:

- It gave people reason to hope because it assured them that

    (1) God's power and goodness would, in the end, prevail over evil; and,

    (2) God would take care of those who remained faithful.

- John's purpose was also to encourage the people to remain faithful and to demonstrate their beliefs, not just with words, but with their lives. Faithful acts of love and service certainly speak louder than words of faith.

15 Was the Book of Revelation unique in its own time?

This question is like asking whether video-tapes are unique in our time. Apocalyptic writings were quite common during New Testament times.

16 So why haven't we heard of other apocalyptic writings?

People who have studied ancient cultures and writings that existed during the time of the New Testament would tell us that there were hundreds of examples of apocalyptic materials. However, few of these other apocalyptic writings were considered important enough by the early church to be included in the Old or New Testaments.

17 But if Revelation is an example of apocalypse, why does John call his vision a *prophecy*?

In Revelation 1:1-3, John says:

> The revelation of Jesus Christ, which God gave him to show his servants what must soon take place; he made it known by sending his angel to his servant John, who testified to the word of God and to the testimony of Jesus Christ, even to all that he saw. Blessed is the one who reads aloud the words of the *prophecy* [italics

added], and blessed are those who hear and who keep what is written in it; for the time is near.

While John doesn't claim to be a prophet, he does refer to his vision as a prophecy. When most people today think about the word *prophecy*, they think about the ability to foretell the future. In common understanding, a prophet is someone who can see into the future or someone to whom God has revealed the future. But that popular view is not really the way prophecy works in the Bible.

18 Q So if prophets didn't predict the future, what did they do?

True prophets, in the finest sense of the Old Testament term, came to speak the word of God to God's people to hold them accountable to God's law and to call them to repentance. The prophets preached against immorality and injustice in any and every form. Without compromise or regard for their own safety, they called people to lead righteous and faithful lives. God's prophets came to a particular people at a particular time. When they did make a "prediction" about what would happen to Israel, it was intended for an immediate future, not some time hundreds of years distant.

So is the Book of Revelation prophecy—either in the biblical sense or in the popular sense?

John did not write the Book of Revelation for our time, nearly two thousand years later. Rather he wrote for his own people, his own time. He believed that the persecutions they were facing were sure signs of the beginning of the end. A new day was coming—and soon! God would dramatically vanquish evil; and the reign of God, of goodness and peace, would begin. John's prophecy was for the particular time and a particular people. However, like that of the biblical prophets, the message was one of calling people to accountability: In order to be a part of God's reign, the people needed to remain faithful to God in the face of persecution.

Was Revelation affected by what was happening in the world when it was written?

Yes. The religious world of the first century was like a packed mall of options and possibilities, everything from the calm and commonplace to the eerie and bizarre. The rich extremes of possibilities certainly influenced the tone and content of the writing. But more important, most people at this time had grown to worship the emperor. Christians, who rejected such worship, were beginning to face persecution, imprisonment, or death. The specter of persecution also influenced the writing.

21 What was the world like then?

In some ways, the world of the first century was not much different from our own. The crises and chaos of the time made many people think that dramatic, cosmic events were about to take place that would bring an end to the world as they knew it. Plenty of attention was given to talk and speculation about what might happen at the end of the world. Even in our modern world, dramatic political events or natural disasters make people start talking about how the end is near.

22 Were there other influences I should know about?

The influence of the old Persian Empire was powerful in the ancient Middle East at the time of the first century. A belief system called *dualism* was ever present. According to this set of beliefs, powerful forces of good and evil fight a cosmic battle with each other. Every decision for good or evil tips the balance of power in one direction or the other. The ancient Persians also held strong beliefs about revelatory experiences, angels and demons, and great end-time battles. They even talked at length about a deceiving power of evil named *Shaitin*, which seems to correspond rather closely to the concept of Satan.

23

What did the people at the time of Revelation think the universe was like?

Scholars have a special name for any understanding of how the universe is constructed. They call this a *cosmology* (which basically means "the way the cosmos or universe is put together"). The most prominent cosmology that appears in the world of the Bible (and in a number of other ancient cultures) has come to be called the three-tier or three-level universe. In this belief, the cosmos was created with three levels: heaven, earth, and the underworld. The firmament overarches the flat surface of the earth like a huge dome. It holds

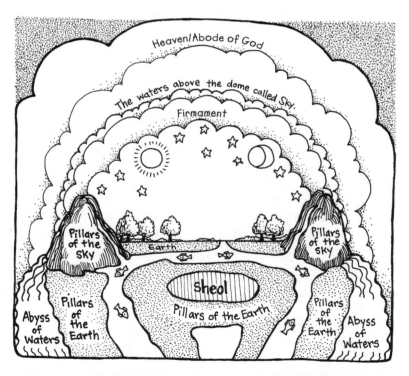

back the heavenly ocean and supports the abode of God. Beneath the earth's surface lie the waters of chaos, which continually threaten to engulf the world in chaos. *Sheol,* the realm of the dead, is located in the depths of this watery deep.

In this way of looking at things, that which is "up" is good and positive; that which is "down" is negative. Even today we are influenced by this idea that heaven and good are up, while hell and evil are down.

24 Q Where is God located in this view of the world?

A The place of God was somewhere just beyond the firmament. It was believed that God was close enough to observe all that was going on in the world. Many believed that the New Jerusalem was constructed in this place of God, and then would descend through the heavens to earth. As an "aside," ancient people believed that a tower could be built from earth to God's place. Remember the story of the tower of Babel (Genesis 11:1-9)? Plot the action of the Book of Revelation with the three-tier concept, and you will clearly see its presence as a backdrop. Look at the Creation account in Genesis, and you can see how far back in biblical history this view of the world goes.

25 Q Has the Book of Revelation always been controversial?

A In fact, the word *controversial* is probably not strong enough! The book was a continual source of debate, argument, and confusion throughout the first hundred years of its existence. Christian leaders of great faith, who were capable of agreeing and working together on many critical matters, often found themselves at odds about what to do with this book. Some leaders felt that the extreme images and visions of the book were more confusing than helpful. On this side of the debate, there was a strong feeling that the negatives far outweighed any positives; it would be better if Revelation simply got lost. Other leaders believed that the book served the important purpose of calling people to new hope in a time of persecution and pain. They felt it had a universal quality that would make it important to future generations.

26 Q Who decided that Revelation should be part of the Bible?

A During the first two centuries of Christianity, wide-ranging discussions were moving in the direction of creating a canon of Christian Scriptures that have ultimately become what we know as the New Testament. The term *canon* describes those Scriptures that came to be approved, certified, and accepted by the leadership of Christianity. Some books were obviously essential and fully acceptable to all parties involved in the discussions. The Gospels and the writings of Paul were agreed upon. Other gospels, or accounts of the life and ministry of Jesus, were considered to be *heretical*, that is, they taught something contrary to what the church believed. Those writings were not included. Revelation was finally accepted in 397 A.D. at the Synod of Carthage as part of the Christian canon.

27 Q So, how did the Book of Revelation finally get into the Bible?

A The Book of Revelation posed a deep problem. Some elements—the strange visions and images—were not attractive to some people. However, the key messages of the power and ultimate triumph of God over evil were seen as indispensable truths that needed to be proclaimed. Also valued was the message the letters to the seven churches at the beginning of Revelation contained: Faith must be demonstrated by actions.

28 Q Why is it important to discuss the Book of Revelation today?

A We need to reaffirm the most important messages of the book:

- First, people have reason to hope. Revelation bears powerful witness to the fact that in the end God's loving goodness will prevail over all evil and that God will take care of those who remain faithful.

- Second, just like the Christians of John's time, we need to focus on a faith that is lived out in acts of love and service. Revelation calls Christians to a life of radical Christian commitment. This message is as relevant and vital for us today as it was for the first-century Christians for whom the book was originally written.

29 | Is there another good reason to study Revelation?

YES! When we learn about the Book of Revelation, we lessen the likelihood of being deceived, misled, or manipulated by its content or by persons who would use it wrongly. We fear the unknown; so if we don't understand Revelation, then we are more likely to be afraid of it. There is enough real fear about the negative directions that the world is heading without adding "possible" interpretations of Revelation to the list. Once a person understands the book's images and strange symbols, gains insight about why it was written, and becomes comfortable with its unique style, then it is easier to see the central truths of Revelation.

30 | Do I have to believe "one way" about the Book of Revelation in order to be a Christian?

Absolutely not! A person does not have to believe one certain way about the visions, images, or signs in the Book of Revelation in order to be a Christian. Even more important, a person does not have to get involved in linking the images in Revelation with certain historical events or personalities. Such attempts are simply irrelevant to the book's message for Christians today.

31 **Is this book going to answer all of my questions about the Book of Revelation?**

Of course not. No one book or teacher can answer all of the questions people have about the Book of Revelation. Like any great mystery, Revelation always retains a depth that no one can completely fathom. Anyone who claims to understand the Book of Revelation completely and to have all the answers is not being realistic. This book is written to support you as you search out the answers for yourself.

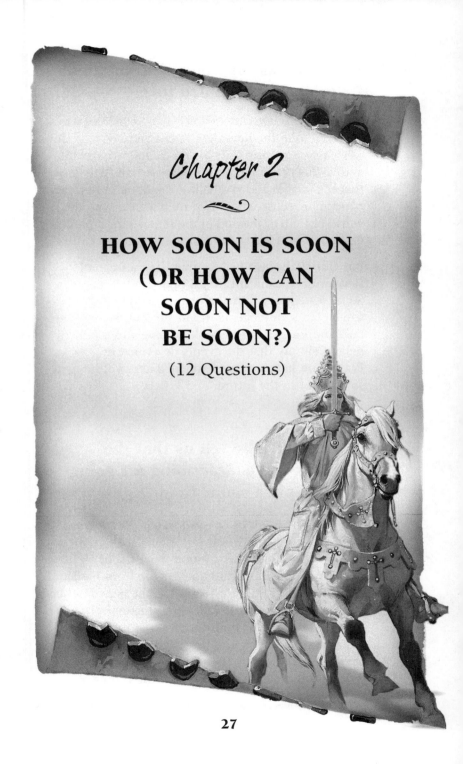

Chapter 2

HOW SOON IS SOON (OR HOW CAN SOON NOT BE SOON?)

(12 Questions)

27

Who was the book of Revelation originally intended for?

First, we can answer what we believe was John the Revealer's intention in writing. John wrote primarily for the people around him and for his present and immediate future. This means that the images and symbols of the Book of Revelation make more sense when they are matched with the world of John at the end of the first century than they do in our world at the end of the twentieth century.

But Christians also believe that the message of Revelation was meant for all times and all peoples. Some readers try to make connections between persons, places, and events in our present day with symbols and images in the Book of Revelation. Others believe simply that the events described in Revelation have not yet happened and will happen sometime "in the future."

Doesn't John tell us that the events he is describing are going to happen soon?

The Book of Revelation has two distinct "bookends"—an introduction and conclusion that wrap around what the book has to say. Revelation 1:1-3 functions as the front bookend while Revelation 22:6-21 serves as the back bookend. Revelation begins with a blessing statement that promises reward for both those who proclaim the material in the book and those who hear it. Such blessing statements were common in apocalyptic writing. John clearly believes that the things he describes will take place in the immediate future. He uses phrases like: "what must soon take place" (1:1) and "for the time is near" (1:3). John continues to emphasize the immediate future in the conclusion. Here he uses the phrases "must soon take place" (22:6); "behold, I come quickly" (22:7); "for the time is at hand" (22:10); "see, I am coming soon" (22:12), and "surely I am coming soon" (22:20).

34   What does it mean when Revelation says "soon" and "near at hand"?

In each instance, language scholars conclude that the force of the Greek language is clear and unmistakable. The words that translate "soon," "near," "quickly," and "at hand" all mean immediately. These are words that describe events that are hours, days, or at most, weeks away. Consider this example: When an airplane is preparing to land, the flight attendant will say, "We are preparing to land. Stow any materials under the seat. Bring your seat to the full, upright position. We will be landing shortly." She doesn't mean two days from now or even two hours from now. She means shortly! The words used in the Book of Revelation carry this same sense of urgency. Clearly, the Book of Revelation stresses the immediate future.

35

How does "sealing up the scroll" fit into what John means when he says "soon"?

Revelation 22:10 is critical for understanding what John means when he says "soon." The text literally reads: "Do not seal up the words of the prophecy of this book [the Book of Revelation], for the time is near." In apocalyptic writing, it was not unusual for some type of prophetic figure to make predictions about the future. These prophecies would then be written down, sealed up for safe keeping, and—after a period of time—unsealed. If the predictions had come true, the validity of the prophetic figure would be confirmed, and additional proclamations would be believed and trusted. So, why would John give the unique instruction not to seal up the scroll on which the predictions of the Book of Revelation are written? There can only be one logical answer: The events described will take place so soon that there is no time and no need to seal the scroll.

36

How does this strange talk about not helping ungodly or unclean people help us understand what John means by "soon"?

When you read Revelation 22:11, it may surprise you. Those people who are described as "righteous" and "holy" are encouraged to hold on to the character of their faith. But that's not the surprising part. What surprises us is that John tells those who are described as "filthy" or "unjust" to simply remain in that condition! This certainly does not sound like what we would expect to hear from the Bible! We would expect the Bible to tell spiritually "filthy" and "unjust" people to repent, change their lives, and begin to live the life that God intends. How could John suggest otherwise? Again, there is only one logical answer: There is not enough time for them to change unless they do it immediately! The end is too near at hand.

37 Can't God's timing be different from human timing?

In response to John's emphasis on "soon," "quickly," and "near at hand;" some people have suggested that the contradiction can be explained by the difference between God's time and human time. Since the events depicted in the Book of Revelation—the end of time—did not take place during John's life or during the past two thousand years, some people have reasoned that God must have a different time frame. According to this argument, "soon" must mean two different things for God and for human beings. This approach has been used to talk about other time frames in the Bible. For example, people who have tried to match evolutionary science with the Creation account in Genesis have suggested that it occurred in seven days, just like the Bible says, but that a day from God's perspective could be billions and billions of years.

Does the Bible say anything about God's time being different from our time?

In Psalm 90:4 the Bible says, "For a thousand years in your sight / are like yesterday when it is past, / or like a watch in the night." The writer of Second Peter draws on this image from the psalmist when he says, "But do not ignore this one fact, beloved, that with the Lord one day is like a thousand years, and a thousand years are like one day" (2 Peter 3:8). The writer of the psalm uses this image to help us imagine what eternity is like, not to give us a "time yardstick" that literally equates one day for God to a thousand years for human beings.

Isn't it dangerous to picture God telling John one thing when God is actually thinking something else?

Imagine someone borrows money from you. "Please let me borrow fifty dollars," he says. "I will pay you back soon." So you loan him the money, and a few days pass. Now you need the money back; so when you meet him at the mall, you ask to be paid back. "Oh, don't worry," he says, "I'll have it for you soon." Weeks pass, then months, and he still has not repaid your money. When you ask him for an explanation, all that he says is that his understanding of soon and your understanding of soon are not the same. "When I said soon," he argues, "I meant thirty years. Thirty years is soon to me." How would you react? Wouldn't you feel tricked and betrayed? Would you ever trust your friend again? When we say soon, we mean soon as it is understood by any reasonable person in any reasonable situation. So for God to say in effect, "Oh, yeah, I told John soon, but I really meant thousands of years," creates serious problems for us. At best, God would have been unfair to John by not helping him understand exactly what "soon" meant. At worst, God tricked and confused John. Why would we want to believe that when God said soon, God meant anything other than what we mean when we say soon?

40 So why didn't the stuff John describes happen soon?

This question assumes that the events described in the Book of Revelation *did not* take place. Some would suggest that they have. "But," it is argued, "the Battle of Armageddon, the Great White Throne Judgment, and the New Jerusalem descending through a new heaven to a new earth hasn't occurred. Why didn't these things happen, especially if God told John that these events would take place soon?" Surely, people—especially people of faith—would not feel comfortable with answers such as "God couldn't make it happen," or "The power of evil was more than God could defeat." Such answers don't match our understanding of God's power.

41 **Q** **But you still haven't answered my question. Why didn't the stuff John describes happen soon?**

A Is there another possibility? Is it possible that God told John that the time was "near at hand," but then decided to give his creatures and creation another chance? "What?" you say, "God's mind can't be changed!" On the contrary, the Bible is full of examples where God gives a person, city, or nation a chance to repent and do what God expects. This is certainly the explanation offered in Paul's letters: God has delayed the Second Coming to give more people the chance to give their lives to Jesus Christ. Could it be that God really intended to end the world soon and revealed that to John, but that God, in infinite mercy, decided to move to a new plan? If we believe that God is love, such a conclusion is not contradictory or inconsistent. God's love may have prevailed over this decision to bring creation to an end.

42 **Q** **So will the world really end the way God revealed to John it would almost 2,000 years ago?**

A In other words, can the Book of Revelation continue to be used as a blueprint for events that will occur at some time in the future? And if that's true, should we be looking for signs of the end in the events that surround our lives? God is God, and God can do anything God desires. That means that God can be as forgiving as God wants to be, and give humans as many "second chances" as God wants to give! True faith recognizes God's absolute and total openness to determine future events in any way God might choose. If we see Revelation this way, we have even more reason to hope for the redemption of creation. Our job is to respond to the central messages of Revelation that give us that hope—God will prevail in the end and will take care of those who are faithful. We should concentrate on living out our faith, rather than attempting to flawlessly predict the future based on the symbols of Revelation.

43 But should we be looking for signs of the end times?

Obsessive searching for signs of the end times distracts us from doing what the Book of Revelation calls us to do—living our faith. Differences about the interpretation of the Book of Revelation have been the occasion for many battles in the church, which is inconsistent with God's desire for people to live in unity. Whether or not we can match specific persons, places, and events with the vision described in the Book of Revelation, God's power and goodness will prevail over evil in the end. God will take care of those who are faithful. We can't allow these great truths to be lost or compromised by worry about the "weird signs" in Revelation. Instead, let us be concerned about what it means to be faithful!

Chapter 3

THE PLAYERS: GOOD GUYS, BAD GUYS, BEASTIE BOYS AND GIRLS

(42 Questions)

44 **Who was the angel who shows John his vision?**
(Revelation 1:1)

While the Book of Revelation never tells us who the angel is, the character identified as "his angel" in Revelation 1:1 and the key angelic figure who converses with John the Revealer at the end of the Book of Revelation has traditionally been considered to be Gabriel.

45 **How did people think about angels during John's time?**

In the religions of the ancient Middle East—the Holy Land—belief in angels was part of their tradition. Not everyone believed in angels, but most people certainly did. The writer of the Book of Revelation unquestionably believed in angels, and they have a prominent place in his writings. Angels make some appearances in the Old Testament; and while angels are not a key concept in the teachings of Jesus, by the end of the first century, belief in angels was commonplace. Many people came to believe that different angels had responsibility for different regions of the world. Angels were mediators between God's heavenly court and earth. They were messengers who carried God's word to people, then carried information about the lives and actions of people back to God.

In the letters to the seven churches (Revelation 2:1–3:22), John writes to the angels of each of the churches. This fact may suggest that John believed that each of the seven churches had an individual, local angel watching over it. Others have suggested that John is addressing either leaders in each of the churches or the church itself.

46 Q Who is the Son of Man? (*Revelation 1:12-20*)

Early in the Book of Revelation the Son of Man appears in all his glorious splendor. He is robed to his feet and has a gold belt around his waist. His hair is like snow-white lamb's wool and his eyes burn with fire. His feet are like polished brass and his voice like the rush of mighty waters. He comes to unlock the secret of the seven lampstands and the seven stars for John. Throughout the Gospels, Jesus is referred to as the Son of Man. If that were not enough to identify him, Revelation gives us the clue that makes it clear that this is Jesus. The Son of Man says, "Do not be afraid; I am the first and the last, and the living one. I was dead, and see, I am alive forever and ever." The Son of Man is Jesus Christ, the one who could not be conquered by death.

47 Q Who are the twenty-four elders? (*First appearance, Revelation 4:4*)

God's throne is surrounded by twenty-four smaller thrones on which sit twenty-four "elders." Because they are dressed in white robes and wear gold crowns, they are most often seen as those who have survived persecution through faith and perseverance and have won the victory. Some would suggest that if we add the twelve disciples (the new faithful) with the twelve tribes of Israel (the old faithful), we get twenty-four. In this case the elders would represent the faithful from all generations.

48 **Are there any good beasts?**
(First appearance,
Revelation 4:6b-10)

As a matter of fact, there are. In God's throne room, we find four creatures. The first is like a lion; the second like an ox; the third had a human face; and the fourth was like an eagle in flight. Each of the creatures has six wings and is covered with eyes inside and out. In John's time these creatures were meant to be symbols of the created order. The lion represents the wild animals; the ox, domesticated animals; the creature with the human face represents human beings; and the eagle in flight, the creatures of the air. Their job is to sing a never-ending song of God's glory and honor.

49 **Who is the "Lamb" prominently featured throughout the Book of Revelation?**
(First appearance, Revelation 5:6)

Without question, the Book of Revelation refers to Jesus Christ as the Lamb. New Testament scholars can trace the evolution of words that were used in the early stages of Christian faith to talk about Jesus. In the earliest stage, expressions such as "Son of Man" were used to describe someone who was God's prophet or unique messenger. In a middle stage, expressions such as "Son of God," "Lord," or "Christ" came into use. As the church and its faith matured toward the end of the first century, descriptions of Jesus that called to mind the idea of God's saving grace became popular. Among these were the expressions "Savior" and "Lamb of God."

50 Why a lamb? Why not, say, a lion?

As John weeps because there was no one worthy to open the scroll containing the purposes of God, one of the twenty-four elders tells him that the "Lion of the tribe of Judah, the Root of David, has conquered" and can therefore open the scroll. But when John looks up, he sees a slaughtered lamb, not a lion, on the throne!

The images of the "Lion of Judah" and the "Root of David" were traditional references pointing to the coming of the Messiah. Most Jews had been expecting a Messiah who would come in power and might to conquer their enemies and establish a new kingdom. But with Jesus' entry into Jerusalem and his death, these traditional messianic expectations were turned upside down: He conquered not by might, but rather through the power of self-sacrificial love. It is the image of a lamb, rather than a lion, that is used to describe the Messiah.

The concept of the lamb has roots in ancient Judaism. In a traditional Jewish religious festival, a goat was used as a sacrifice. The act was symbolic of destroying the obstacles that separated human beings from God. This goat—better known as a scapegoat—

symbolically had the sins of the people placed upon it. The goat was then driven into the wilderness. The idea was that the people's sins had been driven away, and a new beginning with God had been established. It was also common for a lamb to be presented for sacrifice at the Temple as a "sin offering," a way of asking God for forgiveness. Christians began to see Jesus in these terms. He was the Lamb who had taken upon himself the sins of the world. By taking the sins of humankind upon himself, the obstacles between humans and God are destroyed—humanity is *atoned*, made "at one" with God—and new life is possible.

51 Does the Book of Revelation change this lamb idea in any way?

The Book of Revelation makes a powerful transformation in the way the "Lamb of God" is portrayed. No longer is the lamb a poor, helpless creature. The lamb also represents the triumphant presence of God, who wars against evil and drives it from the world. The lamb becomes the earthly embodiment of the power of God! How wonderfully ironic that the placid, gentle lamb becomes the agent of God's triumph. But this power comes not from strength or force, but rather from self-sacrificing love. Christ's triumph over death and the forces of evil is accomplished not by might, but rather by the giving of his own life.

52 **Who are the four horsemen of the apocalypse?**
(Revelation 6:1-8)

In ancient Palestine, mounted riders were associated with power and might; and almost anytime a horse cavalry showed up in battle, the odds of destruction greatly increased. Notice the dramatic way that each subsequent rider is more awful-sounding and destructive in its power than the last.

- A white horse simply goes out to conquer. Some readers have mistakenly interpreted this symbol as representing the Messiah. But the rider of this horse seeks to win victory by forcing others to submit. Some scholars suggest the rider might be a symbol for the emperor Domitian, who was persecuting the Christians at the time of the writing of Revelation.

- A bright red horse goes out to "take peace." Red in apocalyptic imagery is often associated with warfare, strife, and bloodshed. Those who don't submit to the conqueror will experience the chaos and conflict of war.

- A black horse is accompanied by the images of famine and economic disaster, which always follow war and destruction. Black is usually symbolic of the lack of something; and, in this case, it is the lack of food.

- A pale horse finally appears. Actually the horse is more greenish-gray, the color of a dead body. This image would have been profoundly frightening—intentionally so. This horse and its rider, Death, are followed by Hades, which means "the place of the dead." So death follows this rider wherever he goes.

53 Q Who are those people hiding under the altar?
(Revelation 6:9-11)

These are the martyrs who have died in the faith, "slaughtered for the word of God and for the testimony they had given." They call out for God to affirm the truth of the gospel for which they died. Each of them is given a white robe (a symbol of victory in faith) and asked to rest and wait for a little while longer until their number is complete. They will then see that God will vindicate them.

54 Q Who are the 144,000?
(Revelation 7:4-8)

It is not entirely clear who this group of 144,000 is or where the number comes from. The word *sealed* (7:4) is an allusion to Ezekiel 9:4-6 and means that the 144,000 are marked as being under God's protection; they may experience tribulation, but they will ultimately be saved by God. Certainly, this group is made up of faithful followers who have already died and gone on to heaven. Some interpreters say they are people who have been martyred for their faith. Others speak of 12,000 people from each of the twelve tribes of Israel, although by the first century the ability to identify tribal groupings accurately would have been difficult. To say that the number is simply a symbolic reference to the faithful would be sufficient.

55 Q Does that mean that only 144,000 people will be saved and go to heaven?

A Under no circumstances does the Book of Revelation claim that there will only be 144,000 people who will ultimately be saved and go to heaven. In apocalyptic number-symbolism, multiples of ten signify completeness and multiples of twelve represent the people of God (twelve tribes of Israel, twelve apostles). So the writer of the Book of Revelation most likely used this number (which is a multiple of both ten and twelve) to represent *all* the people of God.

56 Q What about these weird locusts that look like horses with riders? *(Revelation 9:1-12)*

A After a star falls from the sky, these hideous creatures are released upon the earth from the bowels of the bottomless pit. Locusts are frequently used as symbols of hard times or invading armies (Joel 1:4-7; 2:1-9). They are like horses equipped for battle. They have human faces, women's hair, lion's teeth, breastplates like iron, stingers like scorpions; and when they fly, they make a noise like chariots rushing into battle. These locusts are given power to torment the earth with plagues for five months.

Five is not a number associated with apocalyptic writing. So why five months? Real locusts that devour crops appear for about five months during spring and summer, cause great loss and havoc, and then disappear. This image is actually intended to give hope to the faithful. Like the locusts, the persecutions that Christians are experiencing will not last forever. Eventually they will pass.

57 *Q* What about these two hundred million horses breathing fire, smoke, and sulphur?
(Revelation 9:17-19)

A At the sounding of the sixth trumpet, the four angels bound at the great river Euphrates are released. They and their cavalry go forth to heap more destruction on the world. The horses' heads are like lions and their tails are like snakes, so they are deadly both coming and going. They snort fire, smoke, and sulfur from their mouths. The fact that Revelation associates the colors with fire and that fire, smoke, and sulfur follow them everywhere they go, emphasizes the total destruction that warfare brings with it.

58 *Q* Who is Satan?
(First appearance, Revelation 2:9)

A The Book of Revelation depicts an intense battle between good and evil. On one side are the "good guys," inspired by and empowered by God. On the other side is God's most powerful adversary, Satan, who leads the forces of evil. By the end of the first century, the idea that Satan was the evil adversary who opposed the power of God and fought for control over the lives of people was an important part of what people believed. Tradition holds that Satan had been an angel, one of God's messengers, who attempted to gain power for himself in heaven and was cast out. Now, as a part of the world, he became an active agent of deception and chaos.

59 Q Does the Bible tell us more about Satan?

A Interestingly enough, the Bible does not give us as many specifics about Satan as one would think. Except for the Book of Revelation, there are not many places in Scripture that give much attention to Satan at all. One is in the story of Job, which plants the idea of Satan as God's adversary. In Zechariah 3:1-2, Satan appears as an "accuser" who challenges God's conclusions. The historical material of the Old Testament, which runs from Genesis and Exodus through Samuel, Kings, and Chronicles, makes little mention of Satan (with the exception of a brief passage in 1 Chronicles 21:1). The prophetic sections from Isaiah and Jeremiah to Malachi have Satan neither as a common or a central theme. Satan is not even very important in the teachings of Jesus, although many people believe that it was Satan who tempted Jesus in the wilderness. Only in the Book of Revelation does Satan take center stage as a major figure in the story, though always as one who has already been defeated.

60 Does Satan have power over us?

Not only does the Book of Revelation teach that the power of God will destroy Satan, death, and evil, but it is one of many places in the Scriptures that tell us that with God's help people already have the power to conquer Satan in their lives. The Bible teaches that people can resist the devil and he will flee from them (James 4:7).

61 What about Satan's armies? (Revelation 19:19)

Satan's armies appear at the end of Revelation to prepare for the battle of Armageddon. They are made up of the forces of evil that oppose the church.

62 What about the serpent and the dragon? (Serpent: first appearance, Revelation 12:9; Dragon: first appearance, Revelation 12:3)

Images of serpents and dragons can be found in the stories of most ancient civilizations of the Middle East. Dragons came to be identified with Satan and the underworld of chaos and evil in Jewish thought. "Leviathan" was one of the names given to the primordial dragon that Yahweh (God) subdued at the dawn of time during Creation. In Jewish apocalyptic literature not included in the Protestant Bible, it was predicted that Leviathan would break loose from his bonds at the end of the present era to suffer a second and final defeat at Yahweh's hand (see Job 3:4b-8 and Isaiah 27:1-2). In the Book of Revelation, the terms *Satan*, *serpent*, and *dragon* are pretty much used interchangeably.

63 Who is the queen of heaven or the woman with child? *(Revelation 12:1-6)*

At the beginning of Chapter 12, a woman appears on the scene. She is robed with the sun, has the moon beneath her feet, and wears a crown with twelve stars. She is pregnant and cries out in the anguish of delivering her child. The great red dragon lies in wait to devour her child as soon as it is born. But God snatches the child away from the dragon, takes him to his throne, and protects him.

Scholars have offered three intriguing interpretations of who this woman could possibly be. Is she the Old Testament giving birth to the New Testament? Is she Mary giving birth to Jesus? Is she giving birth to the church in the world? Or is she all three? Nothing in the Book of Revelation clearly supports any of these conclusions.

We do know that in ancient Babylonia and Persia, there were many stories about a "heavenly queen" who gives birth to a child who was the "son of god" and was a force for goodness and righteousness. In this tradition the child was intended to fight against evil when he grew to adulthood and would ultimately conquer evil. Of course, it would have been in the best interests of any power of evil to try to destroy the divine heir apparent while he was still a baby or a child. In many of these older traditions, the power of evil manifested itself as a dragon or a serpent-like being. So the image of a dragon or serpent pursuing a heavenly queen in order to kill a divine child was well known in the time of John.

Who is the beast?

The earthly symbol of Satan—Satan's earthly champion—was the figure that Revelation refers to as the beast or the great beast.

Who is the beast with the seven heads?
(Revelation 13:1-10)

Revelation uses symbolic pictures to describe the forces who oppose the followers of God. The images and visions grew directly out of the real-life events that surrounded the church at the end of the first century. In the thirteenth chapter of Revelation, the first image is of a beast with seven heads. Some scholars believe this to be a reference to the seven hills upon which Rome was built that, at a distance, look like a seven-headed monster rising up out of the sea. Others believe the seven heads to be a reference to the seven most prominent past rulers of Rome. These seven political leaders were those who had come to power since the time that Rome had grown from a republic to an empire. During that time, there was powerful opposition to Christianity, and the persecution of Christians was beginning. Either way, the beast with the seven heads is linked to Rome. For Christians of that time, the Roman Empire had become the embodiment of evil and the power of Satan in the world.

The beast is described as having ten horns that sparkled like jewels. These horns may be prominent architectural features of the Roman skyline, which, especially at night when they were filled with light, looked like sparkling jewels. This chapter also mentions that blasphemous names are attached to the heads. Many of the Roman emperors insisted on being called by names such as "Son of God" or "Lord" and worshiped. That the Roman emperors were gods would have been a blasphemous idea to the early Christians. And it was precisely because these Christians refused to pay homage to the emperors and acknowledge them as gods, that they were persecuted.

66 Q What is the meaning of the "mortal wound" on one of the heads of the beast? (Revelation 13:3)

John tells us that one of the beast's seven heads seems to have received a death-blow. At first the wound appears to be fatal, but the beast's wound heals; and it prepares to move with an awful vengeance against those who have been faithful to God. The key to understanding this beast is the wounded head. As we have seen, one interpretation is that the heads on the beast (Rome) refer to past rulers of the Roman Empire. Most scholars believe that the wounded head is a symbol for the emperor Nero and that the wounded head comes from a damaging rumor that surrounded his death.

67 What about the three different parts of the beast: body like a leopard, feet like a bear's, and a mouth like a lion's? (Revelation 13:2)

Using animal images to describe groups of people is no new concept at all. Think of the names of some of your favorite athletic teams: the Chicago Bulls, the Florida Marlins, or the Denver Broncos, for instance. Perhaps we think that by embracing an animal's image, we will reflect something of that animal's character. Maybe we will play like Jaguars, Rams, Hawks, or Tigers. The ancient world was no different. Animal imagery had been associated with individuals and groups of people throughout the whole history of human beings.

68 So what do the three animals represent?

Following the death of Alexander the Great, the ancient Greek Empire was divided into four parts: Egypt, Syria, Pergamum, and Macedonia. The four kingdoms fought one another for a long period of time, but gradually an outside empire, Rome, rose to power. Eventually three of the four formerly Greek kingdoms became a primary part of the Roman Empire. Some scholars believe that the three animal parts represent those three kingdoms, which together became a symbol for the Roman Empire itself.

69 What is this beast that rose out of the earth?
(Revelation 13:11-18)

Toward the end of Chapter 13, significant attention is given to a creature who is actually a representative of the first beast who rises from the sea. This beast that rises from the earth has two horns like a lamb and speaks like a dragon.

The main occupation of this second beast is to make the earth and everyone on earth worship the first beast, who represents the Roman Empire. The beast deceives people mainly by performing great and miraculous deeds that gain their attention and impress them with the beast's power.

The beast's deception raises the level of fear that faithful people experience. It was believed that in the last days that there would be representatives of the power of evil who would become leaders of the church by pretending to be true and loyal believers. In fact, they would work like spies, passing destructive information to the evil opposition. The evil ones would, in turn, use that information to destroy the faithful. This deceptive figure is seen as being so good at what he does that most of the faithful are fooled. However, when the veils of phoniness are pulled back, the figure revealed is the Devil. Toward the end of the Book of Revelation, this figure is totally destroyed. The writer of the Book of Revelation may also be referring to an "official priest-hood" who would use these kinds of practices to entice Christians to worship the beast.

70 What is the mark of the beast? *(Revelation 13:16-18)*

One of the most controversial references in the Book of Revelation is the ominous mark of the beast. This one passage has generated more interpretations and misinterpretations than any other part of the book. Markings were commonplace in the first century. Sometimes the marks identified a person as a part of a family or group. Sometimes they were used to keep a person safe from enemies. The Bible has references that go back to marking events as early as Genesis and "the mark of Cain." We know that the lack of the mark in Revelation kept people from buying and selling in the marketplace. People who did not have the mark were forced into the inconvenience, extreme expense, and possible illegality of the "black market." The mark was very much like a license that might be purchased today that would allow a person to conduct business. Without this license or mark, life could become so difficult that giving in to the Romans came to be a better option for many people. We also know that the Romans used systems like this to keep any groups they felt were a threat under control.

71   Who is Nero?

Nero was the emperor of the Roman Empire from A.D. 54–68. He blamed the Christians for many of the problems that the Roman Empire faced. He committed atrocities against the Christians and was responsible for the first great persecution of Christians. Legend has it that both Paul and Peter were executed during the Neronian persecution. It would have been easy for Christians to have seen Nero as their arch enemy and the earthly incarnation of satanic evil. Rumors about his vicious power spread like wildfire through Christian circles.

72   What are the details of this Nero rumor?

The basis for the rumor was that Nero had faked his own death by having himself stabbed in the neck (the wounded head). This "disguise" had allowed him to sneak out of Rome into the back country of Asia Minor, where he was building a gang of murderers and thieves. He would lead these accomplices against Rome, reclaim his throne, and slaughter any and every Christian he could find. Although there was no proof for this rumor, Christians believed it and saw it as the work of Satan.

73 What is the number 666? (Revelation 13:18)

People have become so afraid of the number 666 that they will refuse to pay grocery bills that contain these numbers, reject license plates on cars, and even have street addresses and phone numbers changed. The number has become roughly equivalent to the fears people have about the number 13. With a little bit of scholarly detective work, we find that 666 is another way that the Book of Revelation refers to Nero.

74 Why a number for Nero?

The Latin, Greek, and Hebrew languages did not have numerals in the sense that the English language has a system of numbers separate from letters. Each letter from these languages also had a numerical value and was used to indicate a number. For example, the Roman letters XVIII are equivalent in their system to 18.

So when the Book of Revelation tells us that the number for the beast is a "human number," most scholars believe that this means that the number is a code for a real person. Since each letter also has a numerical value, the letters in a name can also be added up to a get a sum. This way everyone would have both a name and a number. We know that people commonly referred to one another's "number name" because graffiti found on a wall in Pompeii said, "I love her whose number is 545."

75

Q **How do we know that 666 is Nero's "number name"?**

A "Neron Caesar" is the proper way to write the infamous ruler's name in Greek. When this proper name is translated into Aramaic (Hebrew), the number value for it is 666. Interestingly enough, some ancient manuscripts of the Book of Revelation use the number "616" instead of the "666" (your Bible may have a footnote to that effect). If "Neron Caesar" is written in its more common form—"Nero Caesar"—the numerical equivalent would be 616. This makes the case for the link between Nero and 666 that much stronger. However, no one knows for sure. Many people have attempted to suggest other historical figures who could be linked to the number 666. While this might be fun or intriguing to some, it gives us no help in understanding Revelation.

76

Q **Who is the Lamb who goes out to conquer?**
(First appearance: Revelation 17:14)

A There is no question at this point that the drama is gearing up for a gigantic confrontation. The Lamb, as with all other Lamb images in the book, is Jesus. This is the first time that the Lamb/Jesus takes on such an aggressive role; it is almost as if the time has come to put sweetness and kindness aside and to be done with evil. Anyone who has seen the old, traditional format of the nice guy who has had enough, gets fed up, and fights back, can appreciate John's scenario.

77 Q Who are the Lamb's angels? (Revelation 14:6-20)

A Accompanying the Lamb as he goes out are a group of angels. They are not identified by name, but they have the task of announcing the final judgment of the opponents of God. Notice carefully how the announcement of final doom actually precedes any real fighting. This arrangement is completely within the spirit of a great deal of Old Testament prophecy, which sees the promise of God as a "done deal" even before the events described take place. Such is the power of God. The key theme of endurance by the faithful is highlighted in 14:13. Those who endure to the end will be taken care of and ultimately preserved and vindicated by God. The certainty of victory by the angels is the occasion for hope.

78 Q What about the antichrist? (1 John 4:3; 2:18, 22; 2 John 7)

A If there is one concept associated with the Book of Revelation about which everyone knows, it is the antichrist. Would it surprise you to hear that the word *antichrist* is never even mentioned in the Book of Revelation? Many people simply refuse to believe that this is true, but it is. Look up the word in a concordance—you won't find it listed for the Book of Revelation.

79 **But who is the antichrist?**

When the word *antichrist* is used by the people who associate it with the Book of Revelation, it refers to a great and powerful leader who will work to spread universal evil throughout the world at the end of time. However, Christ's return ultimately defeats this malicious leader. Whenever some villainous figure comes on the world scene, he usually gets accused of being the "antichrist." The list has included people such as Adolph Hitler, Joseph Stalin, the Ayatollah Khomeini, and Saddam Hussein.

80 **So where does the idea of the antichrist come from?**

The term appears briefly in the biblical letters of First John and Second John. First John clearly states that there is not simply one antichrist, but many. And rather than specifically referring to a person, the antichrist is seen as a "spirit of denial" that can be part of every person's life (1 John 4:3; 2:18, 2:22; 2 John 7). In other words, instead of worrying about which great, historical villain is the antichrist who will usher in the end of time, we should be concerned about how there might be a spirit or capacity *within us* that denies Christ or fails to show Christlike love.

81 Who is the great whore of Babylon? (*Revelation 17: 1-14*)

Soon after 600 B.C., the Babylonians began to conquer the nations that surrounded them; and their first sights were set on Israel. Not only did they conquer Israel, but they also destroyed Jerusalem—including the great Jewish Temple built by Solomon. They carried off the best and brightest of the Hebrew community into exile and slavery.

After a hundred years or so, some Jews began to return from Babylonian Exile; but the great glory of Israel would never be fully restored. By the end of the first century, Babylonia was a distant memory as far as world politics was concerned. The great empire had long since fallen to the Greeks, and the Greeks had been replaced by the Romans. But for the Jews (many of whom had become Christians) the memory of Babylon and their exile remained as a symbol of all that was evil and oppressive. Because of this, Babylon becomes another dramatic symbol for Rome in Revelation. This tie to Rome is made clear by the fact that the whore or prostitute rides a scarlet red dragon with seven heads (the seven hills on which Rome is built).

82 But why a whore or a prostitute?

The ancient Jewish image of a prostitute was now taking hold as an image in Christian thinking. Look at the Old Testament prophetic Book of Hosea, and the image comes across with power. To "go whoring," to prostitute yourself, was the dramatic symbol of a person, or even a nation, that had sold itself out religiously and compromised its virtue and righteousness. Not only was Babylon/ Rome a new adversary, but Rome was also a religious "whore" who had squandered virtue and denied justice. The combination of Babylon and whoredom created the most negative picture imaginable in the new Christian thinking.

83 Who is the lone rider on the white horse? (Revelation 19:11-16)

The heavens open up and a lone white horse with a rider appears. His eyes flame like fire. On his head are many crowns and his garment is dipped in blood. From his mouth comes a sharp sword, and he carries an iron rod by which he will rule. We are told that he will tread the winepress of the wrath of God. Behind him follow the armies of heaven clothed in shiny white robes and riding on white horses. We are told that he has written on him a name known to no one but himself, that he is called the Word of God, and that on his thigh are written the words "King of kings and Lord of lords." While some have suggested that this is the same white horse and rider from the "four horse-men" passage, it is clear that this reference is different. This is not the rider who went out "conquering for the sake of conquering." The similarity to the Son of Man images is striking; and when we couple that with the fact that he was called "the Word" and has "King of kings and Lord of lords" written on his thigh, it becomes clear that this is Jesus Christ returning in judgment.

84 Who is the false prophet?
(Revelation 16:13; 19:20; 20:10)

The false prophet comes on the scene as one who can work miracles or empower others to work miracles in order to deceive the faithful. Some link him with the second beast who rises from the earth who is sent to trick Christians into making him a high-ranking official in the church. However, there is little evidence to support this connection. The false prophet is destroyed when he is tossed into the lake of fire, the same fate that persecutors of the people of God will share.

85 Who are Gog and Magog?
(Revelation 20: 7-10)

The nations designated as "Gog" and "Magog" had scandalous reputations as far as apocalyptic legends were concerned. Many attempts have been made to match "Gog" and "Magog" with modern nations or personalities. Gog and Magog appear most prominently in Ezekiel 38 and 39. Ezekiel writes during the time of the Babylonian Exile and links Gog and Magog to the nations who persecuted God's people.

We have seen before that John has used Babylon as a symbol for Rome; so we can assume that Gog and Magog are associated with the Roman persecution of the Christians, if not another symbol for Rome itself. The text describes the two nations as being gathered in numbers "like the sands of the sea." The threat to Jerusalem, the "beloved city," is obvious; but this time Jesus and his followers do not even have to fight. The enemy is quickly destroyed by fire raining down from heaven.

Chapter 4

WHAT'S GOING ON HERE? PLACES AND EVENTS

(22 Questions)

What is the winepress of the wrath of God? *(Revelation 14:17-20)*

Images expressing God's judgment on evil mount with growing intensity throughout Chapter 14. The image of the winepress of the wrath of God goes to the heart of Revelation's message of judgment for those who oppose God's purposes. The winepress of God's wrath is set up outside of the city and is used to drain the juice off the grapes as they are trampled. An angel with a great sickle brings in the "vintage of the earth" (14:19). Under normal circumstances, a sickle would not be used as part of harvesting grapes. Obviously, the grapes would be picked and the vines left for another growing season. In this instance, however, there will be no additional growing seasons: This is the end. In this case it is the one called "Faithful and True," the lone rider of the white horse, who treads the grapes (19:15). For 200 miles the blood flows as high as a horse's bridle. Not a happy picture! But the harvest also involves separating the good from the bad. So this image may also echo the idea of the gathering of the "first fruits" (the best of the harvest that is offered to God). Knowing that God will vindicate the faithful and that they will escape this cosmic winepress would have given persecuted Christians great hope.

Imagery associated with the growing and harvesting of grapes is frequent in the Bible. Jesus often referred to the vineyard and wine as symbols in his teachings. The Old Testament prophets also used these images. For example, Hosea 9:10 compared Israel to grapes in the wilderness, and Jeremiah 25:30 and Amos 9:13 described God's anger with the image of treading grapes.

87 *Q* What Is Armageddon? (*Revelation 16:13-16*)

A Armageddon has come to be seen as the final battle, the last great confrontation between good and evil. The vision of the sixth bowl ends with the forces of good and evil arrayed at "the place called in Hebrew Harmagedon." The Hebrew prefix *har* means mountain or city, and many commentators believe that Harmagedon refers to "the mountain of Megiddo," or the "city of Megiddo." Megiddo was a fortress city located in central Palestine, northwest of Jerusalem. Throughout history this area had been a primary thoroughfare into Jerusalem for invading armies. The hills that stood overlooking the plains protected the city and had often been a "last stand" battle position for the Hebrew armies. If there were any kind of final, cataclysmic battle that involved Palestine and Jerusalem, Armageddon would be seen, especially by the Jews, as the classic, timeless battleground. Although John describes the gathering of the armies of the world for battle, the conflict never actually takes place! The forces of evil are destroyed by God before the battle can begin (19:13).

What is the rapture?
(1 Thessalonians 4:13-18)

When seen in relation to Revelation, some interpret the rapture as the idea that the faithful and true believers of the church will be whisked out of the world before the truly evil and oppressive end times begin. Who hasn't seen one of those bumper stickers that reads: "In case of the rapture, this car will no longer have a driver"? For many people, the thought of being raptured out of the world—or, even worse, of being left behind—is scary.

But the concept of rapture does not come from the Book of Revelation. Only one Scripture in the entire Bible even remotely teaches the idea of a rapture and it is found in 1 Thessalonians. In this passage Paul describes the Second Coming of Christ, an event that he believes will happen any minute rather than in the distant future.

So if the concept of the rapture doesn't come from Revelation, why do so many people associate it with this book?

Although the idea of the rapture does not directly come from the Book of Revelation, it has been linked to Revelation in a variety of ways. First, some suggest that the rapturing moment occurs at the first resurrection (20:5) when the beheaded martyrs (20:4) are taken out of the world. If that is true, then the rapture would only apply to the small number of people who have been killed for their Christian beliefs, rather than to a large number of believers as many interpreters have claimed. Others suggest that the rapture applies to the general resurrection of the dead that precedes the final Great White Throne Judgment (20:11-15). However, the Book of Revelation clearly says that everyone who has died will be judged according to how they have lived, including both "great and small," both Christians and non-Christians, and both good and bad people. By contrast, most accounts of the rapture describe only the good and faithful people as being taken out of the world. This emphasis on the rapturing of good people is nearly always paralleled by an emphasis on the evil people being left behind. Others argue endlessly about other places where the event of the rapture could be inserted in the Revelation timeline. One thing is clear: There is *no* passage in the Book of Revelation that tells us that only the faithful and true Christians will be taken out of the world.

90   What is the great tribulation or great ordeal? (*Revelation 7:14, Daniel 12*)

The great tribulation or great ordeal is a period when unimaginable suffering will be inflicted on those who, at the end of time, remain in the world. Much like the idea of rapture, reference to a period of tribulation occurs in only one verse in the Book of Revelation. It is tied to a concept that is central to the Book of Daniel. That book describes a major cataclysmic event that becomes a key ingredient in the unfolding of God's apocalyptic plan. Different groups within the church continue to speculate about when the great tribulation will occur. Has it already taken place? Will it take place before Jesus returns or after Jesus returns? Will everyone be subject to its ravages or just those who are unfaithful? This is another idea from Revelation that some people attempt to associate with major, negative world events. Whenever a war begins; a world leader dies; or an earthquake, famine, storm, or flood occurs, you can count on someone expressing the belief that this event marks the beginning of the great tribulation.

91 Q What is the marriage feast of the Lamb? (Revelation 19:6-10)

A The marriage feast was an important concept during the first century. When allies came together, faced a common enemy, and won, there would be a great feast. One important reason for the feast was to celebrate victory. But the feast would often go beyond mere celebration. Sometimes a marriage would also take place. This marriage would unite key members of each of the allied nations, tribes, or families. The operative idea was to tie the victors together even more intimately and to cement their alliance through marriage. There was the added, practical idea that people who were kin would be much less likely to fight against each other later. In the Book of Revelation, the symbolic marriage occurs between the Lamb and the Bride of Christ. The Bride of Christ is most often understood to be the "true church," which consists of those faithful believers who endured despite persecution and who accomplished God's purposes.

92   What is the bottomless pit?
(Revelation 9:1; 13:1; 17:8; 20:1)

The bottom tier of the three-tier universe is surrounded by the chaotic waters of the sea. For the people of John's time, this sea was thought to be an infinite abyss, having no bottom or end. Throughout ancient Middle Eastern culture, the sea was closely identified with evil, chaos, calamity, and all of the negative potential in creation.

93   How is Satan bound?
(Revelation 20:2)

The Book of Revelation tells us that an unnamed angel comes down from heaven, binds Satan with a chain, throws him in the bottomless pit, and locks him away. The absence of a titanic struggle between the angel and Satan demonstrates God's absolute, eternal power over Satan and the forces of evil. As far as we can tell, God doesn't find it necessary to send a warrior angel of great reputation (like Michael, for instance) to accomplish this task. Any angel can do the job. This image would have brought great hope to the people of God as they struggled to remain faithful during persecution.

94 Q What happens to the martyrs who have given their lives for the cause of God? *(Revelation 20:4)*

A When the scene shifts back to heaven and the throne of God, we see those who, because of their faith, had been beheaded by the forces of evil. They did not worship the beast or receive the mark of the beast. These faithful martyrs have been brought to life and transported to heaven, although there is no explanation of how this process took place. (See question 88–89 regarding the rapture.) For some cultures beheading was the worst death imaginable because they feared it meant an eternal severing of body, mind, and soul. But when these beheaded martyrs are resurrected, God demonstrates that for the faithful no death is final. John describes these special, faithful ones as reigning with Christ in heaven for the thousand-year period that Satan is locked in the bottomless pit.

95 Q What is the millennium? *(Revelation 20:4-6)*

A This thousand-year period when Satan is bound in the bottomless pit is also called the *millennium*, meaning a "period of a thousand years." During this time, the faithful martyrs will reign with Jesus Christ in heaven (rather than on earth as many believe). But after this period, Satan will be loosed for a short while before the general resurrection and judgment of the dead takes place. At no time during this period is Jesus on the earth. Remember that in apocalyptic writings, numbers nearly always have deeper symbolic significance.

Multiples of ten (100, 1,000, and so forth) symbolize completeness and inclusiveness. So it is likely that the writer of the Book of Revelation was referring to this idea of completion rather than to a literal time period of 1,000 years.

96 Q What happens when Satan is loosed? (Revelation 20:7)

It is important to note that Satan is *let* loose; he does not escape. God is completely in control and can even use Satan for God's own purposes. Satan then enters the world again to deceive humanity. (The most characteristic element of Satan's nature is deception.) Satan also wants to make war against the faithful and the "beloved city" (probably the city of Jerusalem). But as the forces of evil approach the beloved city, fire comes down from heaven and consumes them. In a flash, it is all over. Satan is then thrown into the lake of fire and is not heard from again.

97 Q What is the first resurrection? (Revelation 20:4-6)

Throughout history, Christians have offered many understandings of the first resurrection. Some interpret this as a spiritual resurrection rather than a bodily resurrection of the martyrs. Others suggest that this group is the first to experience bodily resurrection. The first resurrection probably applies only to the martyred (beheaded) faithful who have been brought back to life to reign in heaven with Jesus during the millennium. It would logically follow that a second resurrection of all the other people who have died would need to also take place. (See also Final Judgment, question 100, and second resurrection, question 99.)

98 Q What is the lake of fire? (Revelation 19:20, 20:10-15, 21:8)

The lake of fire is the place of punishment and destruction for those who have been opponents of God's purposes and who have persecuted the faithful. This image is the basis for many of the ideas people have about hell. The lake of fire has been associated with *Gehenna,* a word that had come to symbolize the place of fiery judgment that awaits the wicked.

Gehenna, which literally translates as the "valley of Hinnom," referred to a valley outside of Jerusalem that served as the garbage dump and sewage reservoir for the great city. Fires of sulfur ("brimstone") burned there continually, both to cover a more awful smell and to act as a seal when the sulfur melted and hardened over the trash and sewage. Wild animals and equally wild people lived in the seemingly uninhabitable area surrounding Gehenna. There were even old stories about the most terrible criminals being taken to cliffs overlooking the valley and thrown in. Gehenna was a real-life image of the most terrible place imaginable for the people to whom John wrote. The most horrific scenes of a Stephen King or Clive Barker novel would come nowhere close to capturing what the wild, demonic, fiery pit that Gehenna called to mind for the people of John's time.

99

What is the second death? (*Revelation 2:11, 20:6, 20:14, and 21:8*)

Revelation 20:6 and 20:14 must be read together to understand the second death completely. After Satan is loosed from the bottomless pit, he gathers a great army for the final conflict. But as Satan and his forces surround Jerusalem, the army is consumed by fire from heaven. Then Satan is thrown into the lake of fire, where the beast and the false prophet have already been flung. When the remaining dead are resurrected, those judged unfaithful will also be thrown into the lake of fire, along with Death and Hades. John tells us that their banishment to the lake of fire is the second death: Satan, the forces of evil, and death itself are finally and ultimately defeated and separated from God. The timeline looks like this:

- The First Death: the first series of destructive events, including the persecution of the faithful, the destruction of evil powers, and the bondage of Satan

- The First Resurrection: the bringing to life of the beheaded martyrs who then reign with Christ in heaven for a thousand years

- The Second Resurrection: the bringing to life of all remaining people for the final judgment of God before the white throne

- The Second Death: the ultimate destruction of and victory over Satan and all evil powers and forces

100 Q What is the Final Judgment? (Revelation 20:11-15)

A Without question, the Book of Revelation teaches the concept of a final, ultimate judgment. With great clarity and certainty, John describes a gathering of all the dead for a time of judgment. They all stand before the throne of God and each is judged "according to their works, as recorded in the books" (20:12).

101 Q What happens to Death and Hades? (Revelation 20:14-15)

A In the last verses of Chapter 20, we encounter one of the most thought-provoking and perplexing set of questions in the entire book. The text says that Death and Hades are thrown into the lake of fire. In addition, people who were not found in the Lamb's book of life—the record book of works and deeds by which the dead will be judged—are also thrown into the lake of fire, a point repeated in verse 8 of the next chapter.

But how can Death and Hades be thrown into the lake of fire? John personifies Death and Hades as enemies of humanity and agents of evil because of their power to devour humanity. And where exactly is the lake of fire located? Does it exist in a realm outside the earth as a polar opposite to heaven? Though these are tantalizing questions, the important point is that death and everything associated with it is destroyed. No longer does it have any power over humanity.

102 Q What happens to the earth and the sky? *(Revelation 20:11)*

A Revelation 20:11 tells us: "The earth and sky fled from [God's] presence, and no place was found for them." In the three-tier creation, this means that the upper tier, the firmament or sky, and the middle-tier, the earth itself, cease to exist. (See question 23.) If we take this statement literally, then only the sea or watery deep (which is identified with chaos and evil) and heaven (the place where God is) remain. Be careful here, since many translations use the terms *sky* and *firmament,* and the terms *heaven* and "the place where God is" interchangeably. Clearly, the heaven that disappears is not the same heaven where God is. The absence of the old heaven/sky and the old earth is important for all that will take place in the remainder of the book. It is a "clearing away" to make room for the new heaven and new earth that appears at the beginning of Chapter 21. Because the earth and sky "fled away," some have suggested that the God's judgment is to be so fearsome that not even the earth and sky want to hang around to see what happens next.

103 Q What happens to the sea? (Revelation 21:1)

A Chapter 21 begins with some of the most famous words in the entire Bible: "Then I saw a new heaven and a new earth; for the first heaven and the first earth had passed away, and the sea was no more." Now, with the beginning of Chapter 21, John's tone becomes triumphant and glorious. He is ready to explore the wonderful actions of God that come after the judgment.

By the end of Chapter 20, all that remains of the three-tier creation is heaven (abode of God), the sea, and the lake of fire. The old earth and the old heaven/sky/firmament have ceased to exist. Because the sea represents chaos, rebellion, and disorder, there is simply no room for its existence in the new creation. For the Christians of the first century this would be a message of great promise and hope.

104 Q What is this New Jerusalem? (Revelation 21:1–22:5)

A The New Jerusalem is the place that God constructs in heaven (the place of God in the three-tier creation) for those who have been judged to be faithful followers. It is a symbol for a new age in which persecution no longer exists. The New Jerusalem comes down to earth—but not to the old earth.

John is taken up to a high place on the new earth where he is able to gain a preview of the New

Jerusalem before it settles on its new foundation. He gives us an elaborate description of what the New Jerusalem looks like. John measures the city; it is a perfect cube fifteen hundred miles in height, length, and breadth (21:16). Since the cube was regarded as the most perfect geometric shape in John's time, he uses this image to point to the absolute perfection and symmetry of the city. The city also contains twelve gates, twelve angels, twelve tribes, and twelve apostles. Again, John's intention is to describe the utter splendor of this new paradise, and he uses the number 12 as another way to symbolize its perfection. He also describes the city as being constructed of jewels, gold, jasper, pearls—the most beautiful images he knew.

But even more important than the size or physical characteristics of the New Jerusalem is the idea that God will dwell *with* the people. There will be no more night, no more tears, death, or suffering. No longer will there be a gulf separating God from human beings. God's presence is the source of both light and life in the city.

105 Why is there no temple in the New Jerusalem? (*Revelation 21:22*)

Because the city is filled with the presence of God, there is no need for priests or temples to mediate between God and the people. In fact, the city itself can be described as a temple. John's description of the city as a cube recalls the Old Testament Holy of Holies. Whereas the presence of God was so restricted in the Holy of Holies that the

High Priest alone was allowed to enter once a year, the presence of God in the Holy City will be available to all. Humanity will enjoy complete and immediate fellowship with God.

106 According to Revelation, where will the faithful spend eternity? (Revelation 21:9-26)

If this question were asked on a survey, almost certainly the majority of people would quickly answer, "The faithful will spend eternity in heaven." However, when we follow John's descriptions closely, it becomes clear that the eternal habitation of the faithful will not be heaven in the sense of this original, separate "place of God" described in the three-tier model of creation. The faithful will dwell in the New Jerusalem. John tells us that God will also dwell with the faithful in the New Jerusalem. God's presence is what makes the New Jerusalem a "heavenly place." God has come to spend eternity with the faithful.

107   What about the river of life? (*Revelation 22:1-2*)

A pure, crystal-clear "river of the water of life" flows from the throne of God through the middle of the New Jerusalem. Imagine how powerful the image of a never-ending source of pure, clear water would have been for a people who lived in the desert. God's throne is the source of the river, symbolizing that all life comes from and is sustained by God.

On either side of the river stands a tree of life that bears twelve different kinds of fruit, one during each month of the year. John uses the number 12 to symbolize the complete, life-sustaining power of this tree. The presence of the trees of life echoes the description of Eden in Genesis 2. The leaves of the trees are for the "healing of the nations."

The river and trees create a sense of the eternal, unwavering intention of God to care for faithful people. God's New Jerusalem is not a temporary or momentary undertaking: God will provide for the needs of the faithful through all eternity. For the Christians suffering persecution, this image offered great promise and was a source of hope and reassurance. This description is precisely what a group of faithful believers at a time of great threat and turmoil needed to hear. And this is what we also need to hear today!

JOHN RECEIVES A VISION
Revelation 1:1-2
(Questions 1, 6, and 17.)

~

Altarpiece of St. John the Baptist and St. John the Evangelist

Memling, Hans (1425/40–1494). Right wing; apocalyptic vision of Saint John the Evangelist. 1474–1479. Oak. 176 x 78.9 cm. Memling Museum, Sint-Janshospital, Bruges, Belgium. Photo: Erich Lessing/Art Resource, NY

VISION OF THE HEAVENLY THRONE
Revelation 4:1–5:14
(Questions 48–50)

The Vision of the Lamb
(Apoc.4:6–5:6-8).

Commentary on the Apocalypse by Beatus de Liebana. Spain (Leon), c.950 CE.
M.644, f.87. The Pierpont Morgan Library, New York, N.Y., U.S.A.
Photo: The Pierpont Morgan Library/Art Resource, NY

VISION OF THE LAMB Revelation 5:1-14 (Questions 49–51, 76–77)

~

Adoration of the Mystic Lamb

Eyck, Jan van (c.1390–1441). Detail from the Ghent altarpiece. Cathedral St. Bavo, Ghent, Belgium. Photo: Scala/Art Resource, NY

THE TWENTY-FOUR ELDERS
Revelation 4:4, 10-11; 5:8-14
(Question 47)

∽

The Four and Twenty Elders Casting Their Crowns before the Divine Throne

Blake, William (1757–1827).
ca. 1805. Tate Gallery, London, Great Britain.
Photo: Tate Gallery, London/Art Resource, NY

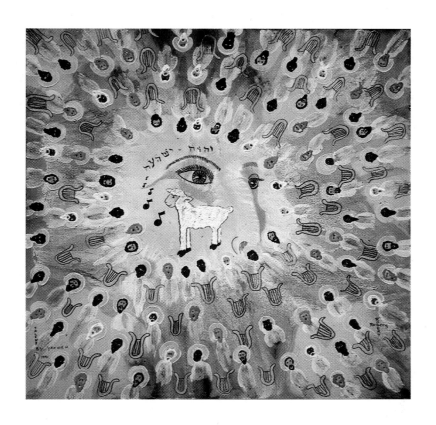

THE LION OF JUDAH
Revelation 5:1-6
(Question 50)

∽

The Lion of Judah

Robert Roberg (b. 1943).
1992. Oil on masonite, 3½ ft. x 3½ ft.
From the collection of the Suzanne Shawe

The Structure of Revelation at a Glance

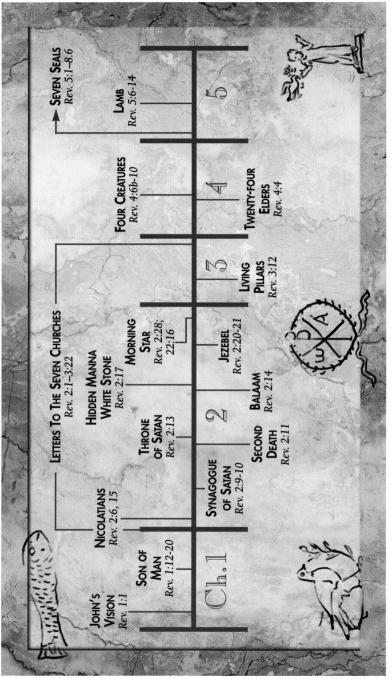

Chart Courtesy of Vinnie Sabatino

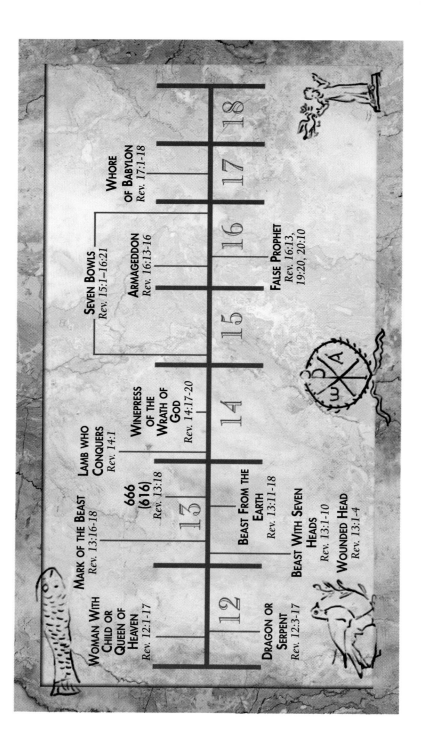

Woman With Child or Queen of Heaven
Rev. 12:1-17

Mark of the Beast
Rev. 13:16-18

666 (616)
Rev. 13:18

Lamb who Conquers
Rev. 14:1

Winepress of the Wrath of God
Rev. 14:17-20

Seven Bowls
Rev. 15:1–16:21

Armageddon
Rev. 16:13-16

Whore of Babylon
Rev. 17:1-18

Dragon or Serpent
Rev. 12:3-17

Beast With Seven Heads
Rev. 13:1-10

Wounded Head
Rev. 13:1-4

Beast From the Earth
Rev. 13:11-18

False Prophet
Rev. 16:13, 19:20, 20:10

12 13 14 15 16 17 18

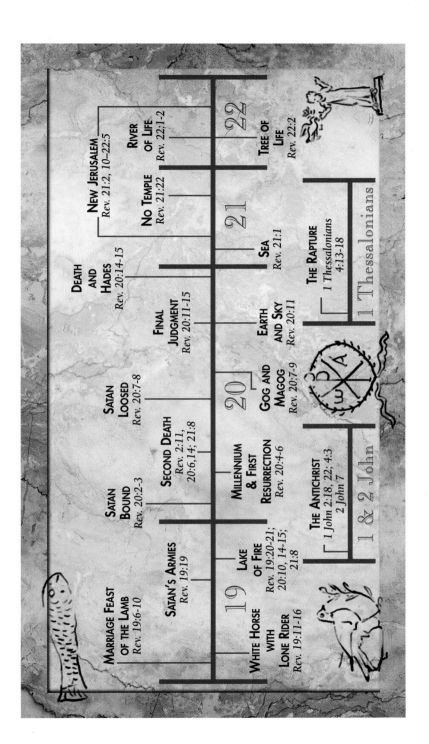

THE FINAL JUDGMENT
Revelation 20:11-15
(Questions 99–101)

~

Last Judgment

Ceiling fresco on the sacristy of the abbey church of Vorau, 1716.
Abbey of the Augustinian Canons, Vorau, Austria.
Photo: Erich Lessing/Art Resource, NY

THE NEW JERUSALEM
Revelation 21:1–22:5
(Questions 104–106)

The Heavenly Jerusalem. The Apocalypse of Angers. No. 80

Bataille, Nicolas (fl.1373–87). Tapestry, 1373-1387. Musee des Tapisseries, Angers, France. Photo: Giraudon/Art Resource, NY

THE RIVER OF LIFE AND THE TREE OF LIFE

Revelation 22:1-2
(Question 107)

John Is Shown the River of Life and the Tree of Life.

Robert Roberg (b. 1943).
1991. Oil and acrylic on wood,
48 x 48 in. (121.9 x 121.9 cm).
From the collection of the artist.

Chapter 5

ARE THESE SEVENS LUCKY OR UNLUCKY?

(28 Questions)

108 Why all these sevens?

The number 7 was often referred to as "the number of perfection." It carries with it the ideas of closure, maturity, and completeness. God created the world in seven days, and we follow that seven-day pattern on our calendars. Perhaps John uses the cycles of seven to indicate that there is a certain perfection to the final actions of God that bring closure and completeness to creation. The re-creation and renewal of the world will happen in successive cycles of seven, echoing God's original creative act. The world will come to a perfect ending.

109 Are numbers important?

In the Book of Revelation (and in other parts of the Bible), numbers are almost always used symbolically. For instance, the number 4 also symbolizes completion. Some think this is because there are four basic directions: north, south, east, and west. Other than seven, 3 is the number most often thought of as sacred. The most obvious example of this would be the Trinity: Father, Son, and Holy Spirit. (Remember, creation has three tiers; and "the beginning," "the middle," and "the end" make up the three parts of whatever must happen in order for it to be complete). Note that three added to four gives us seven!

110 How many sevens are there?

The pattern of seven occurs throughout Revelation. Some examples include:

- Seven letters to seven churches: 2:1–3:22
- Seven seals: 6:1–8:6
- Seven trumpets: 8:7–11:19
- Seven bowls of wrath: 15:1–16:21

111 What is important about the letters to seven churches?

By the end of the first century, there was a great deal of confusion among second generation Christians about the meaning of faith. This confusion was beginning to threaten the very existence and credibility of the church. Even true believers can become confused and lose their way. According to Jesus, belief by itself was not enough; belief had to be acted out in deeds. A powerful theme of Jesus' teaching is his focus on faith bearing fruit through action. The seven letters call people back to Jesus' view of faith. The letters repeat the refrain: "I know your works!" How people show their faith in real life actions becomes critical.

112 Q Do other books of the Bible emphasize the importance of acting out one's faith?

A The New Testament books of James and First, Second, and Third John, which were written and used in the early church at about the same time as Revelation, sound out this same theme. James unequivocally states: "Faith without works is dead." The first letter of John is abundantly clear that a person who loves is a child of God and knows God; those who do not love know nothing of God. This statement doesn't simply refer to an emotion, a warm, fuzzy feeling, but rather to love expressed in and through action. Doing deeds of love—not simply thinking and believing how wonderful love is—is the true core of faith.

113 Q Why were these particular churches so important to the early church?

A Look at the map on page 85. The strategic geographical position of these seven churches is critical. They stand at the "bridge point" of the Roman Empire as it moves from Rome into Asia Minor. In addition, the cities represented were prosperous and upwardly mobile. If Christianity really worked in the region of these seven churches, then it could flourish and have an impact on great masses of people.

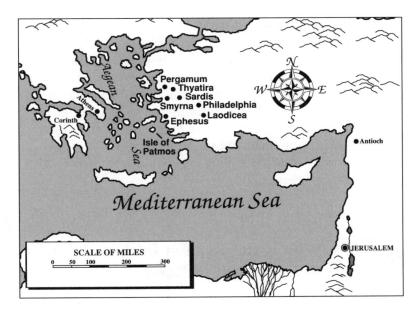

114 What were the people in these churches like?

The people who made up these churches were not much different from us. They had vast potential, but they were not perfect. They struggled to live out their faith in a daily commitment to Jesus just as we also strive to live as followers of Christ.

115 What is the common theme that unites these letters?

A key message of the Book of Revelation is the theme of all these letters: What are you doing in your life as a Christian? According to the Book of Revelation, Christianity is about what

---

we are willing to do in the name of Jesus Christ. Of course, that emphasis doesn't mean that what we say, think, feel, and believe is not important. However, the Book of Revelation stresses that we can think, say, feel, and believe all of the right things, but if we don't *also* do the right things, the rest has little meaning. These letters are bound together by their call to Christians to live the faith no matter what kind of opposition they experience from the world around them.

116 Why is the issue of faith and works so important to Revelation?

Let's imagine that a person has become the world's most recognized authority on raising children. Every week, he teaches the psychology of child-rearing at a renowned university. This professor is frequently asked to come to international conferences and speak on his field of expertise. There are twenty-five books and over a hundred articles about raising children to this professor's credit. Thousands of people have been inspired to be good parents by this work. Yet, when the professor goes home—if at all—he is abusive to his own children. What would you think? He has all the right ideas and proclaims these ideas with passion, but he does not practice them. He lacks integrity and credibility. In each of the letters to the seven churches, John declares, "I know your works!" He believed that our actions are the true witness of one's faith. A belief, no matter how passionately proclaimed, does not mean much until acted upon.

How is this message communicated through the letters to the seven churches?

The letters praise each church for what it does right and criticizes it for what it does wrong. The problems these churches experienced are similar to the problems churches experience today, as you will see.

What does the first letter say? *(Revelation 2:1-7)*

The first letter is addressed to the church at Ephesus. They have done a good job of living out their faith in times of persecution, and they place a strong emphasis on "being pure." But their desire for purity has led them to become self-righteous in their demands on others. They have become more judgmental and less loving each day. The challenge for the people at the church in Ephesus is to endure the time of persecution without losing their capacity to love.

Who are these Nicolaitans mentioned in the first letter? *(Revelation 2:6)*

Scholars are not sure. Irenaeus, a leader of the early church, suggested that they followed a man named Nicolaus of Antioch. Nicolaus taught a different understanding of

Christianity called *gnosticism*. One of the main features of gnosticism is the belief that the world is divided into two spheres, the spiritual and the material. Those things belonging to the spiritual realm are seen as good, while those belonging to the material realm are believed to be basically evil. Although humans belong to this material realm, they also contain a spiritual spark that longs to break free of the body and be reunited with the spiritual. Gnostics also believed that only certain special people can have access to the spiritual knowledge necessary to understand God's purposes.

It is not hard to see why the church rejected this idea early in its history. The gnostic belief that the created world is fundamentally evil was at odds with the Christian belief in the goodness of creation. And this dualism led to serious questions about the nature of Christ. Gnostics denied that God, who is pure spirit, would have ever entered the material realm as a human—Christ only *appeared* to be human. Again, this was in direct contradiction to the Christian belief that Jesus Christ was both fully human and fully divine.

120 What does the second letter say? (*Revelation 2:8-11*)

The second letter addresses the church at Smyrna. This church has endured severe persecution, and they are having trouble keeping their hope alive while they are being thrown into prison and "put to the test." Their challenge is to remember that no matter what they face, God will be victorious. The letter reminds them that if they keep the faith they will receive "the crown of life" and escape the second death.

121 Q What is the "synagogue of Satan" mentioned in this letter?
(First appearance: Revelation 2:9-10)

A This notorious passage has often been used to inspire hatred toward Jews. It is likely that some (not all) of the Jews in Smyrna were participating in the persecution of the Christians there. This reference is to people who intentionally deceive. Anyone who understands this to refer to "all Jews" is wrong.

122 Q What does the third letter say?
(Revelation 2:12-17)

A The third letter addresses the church at Pergamum. The membership of the church was a mix of both faithful and unfaithful people. The letter commends the many members who had stood strong in their Christian faith, even though they lived in a city known for its practice of emperor worship and for its temples to many different gods. At least one member, named Antipas, had died for his faith. They are called to task because some of them are listening to false teachers, especially those practicing gnosticism. (See question 119.)

123 **Q** **What does this letter mean when it talks about the throne of Satan being located in Pergamum?** *(Revelation 2:13)*

A A temple dedicated to emperor worship had been built in Pergamum by the emperor Augustus in 29 B.C. Most likely this "throne of Satan" refers to this temple. But it could have also been a reference to the numerous temples to pagan gods that were located in the city.

124 **Q** **Who is this Balaam mentioned in this letter?** *(Revelation 2:14)*

A In the Old Testament, King Moab hired Balaam to curse the Israelites as they crossed over into the Promised Land. Most scholars believe that in the Book of Revelation Balaam symbolizes all of the false teachers to which the people of Pergamum fell prey.

125 **Q** **What are the "hidden manna" and the "white stone"?** *(Revelation 2:17)*

A Those who stand firm against persecution and false teachers will be given "hidden manna" and a "white stone." Both symbols seem to be linked to rewards for enduring in the faith. The image of hidden manna recalls the manna, or bread from heaven, that God provided for the people of Israel during their long journey through the desert to the Promise Land (Exodus 16:14-15, 31-35) This *hidden* manna symbolizes God's promise to sustain the faithful.

The white stone is a bit more curious. In some places in the ancient world, a white stone served as a ticket to gain admission to a particular society or group. Possession of a white stone was a sign that you had been invited and that you belonged in the group. In this context, the white stone represents an admission into heaven or into an age free of persecution. For those who had the white stone it was an identification that they belong to Christ.

126 *Q* What does the fourth letter say? (*Revelation 2:18-19*)

A The fourth letter addresses the church at Thyatira. While this letter is the longest of the seven, the church itself is the smallest and least influential of the seven. It praises the members for their love, faithfulness, fortitude, and good service and for the progress they have made. However, there is a strong element of immoral behavior at this church, led by a woman referred to as Jezebel. Although the letter uses the word *fornication*, it is probably meant as a reference to false worship and idolatry rather than to sexual immorality.

127 **Q** **So, who is this woman named Jezebel?**
(Revelation 2:20-21)

A John identifies this woman "who calls herself prophet" (2:20) with Jezebel, the Phoenician queen of King Ahab (1 Kings 16 and following). Jezebel corrupted the faith of the Israelites by introducing the worship of Baal, the god of her homeland. Because the Old Testament Jezebel was linked to sexual immorality, over the years she has become a symbol for the temptations of sexual sin. But in this context, she most likely symbolizes the people of Thyatira's connection to false gods of foreign origin.

128 **Q** **What is the "morning star" mentioned in this letter?**
(Revelation 2:28)

A The morning star is one of the most beautiful and abiding images in apocalyptic literature. It is a symbol of the glorious reward awaiting those who persevere in the cosmic struggle between good and evil. We know the morning star as the planet Venus, which often appears just above the horizon in the early morning hours. The first star, appearing just after the dawn of a new and glorious day, awaits the faithful after their work on earth is completed. John later applies this image to Christ (22:16). The reward of the faithful will be to share in the victory of Christ and to enjoy his presence.

129 Q What does the fifth letter say? (Revelation 3:1-6)

A The fifth letter addresses the church at Sardis. Though this church appears to be alive and vital, it is actually spiritually dead. Because of its apathy, the church never brings anything it does to completion or finishes any task that it starts. Just as the city had failed to be vigilant and had been conquered in the past, the church had failed to be watchful and was spiritually unprepared for Christ's return. The letter calls for the church to "wake up" since only a scant few of the Christians at Sardis remain true to God's purposes.

130 Q What does the sixth letter say? (Revelation 3:7-13)

A The sixth letter addresses the church at Philadelphia, praising the members for their steadfast endurance in the face of difficult times. The letter commends them for standing fast even though they "have but little power." John challenges them to continue the witness that they have already begun.

131 Q What is the pillar that this letter talks about?

A Have you ever heard anyone say, "She's a pillar of the church"? This is where that idea comes from. If the Christians at Philadelphia endure through persecution, they are promised that they will become living pillars in the temple of God. One confusing aspect of this reference is that we are later told that the New Jerusalem will have no temple in it. One way of resolving this contradiction is to understand the temple not as a literal building, but rather as a symbol of the people of God.

132 Q What does the seventh letter say? (Revelation 3:14-22)

A The seventh letter addresses the "lukewarm" church at Laodicea. Laodicea was a city of great wealth with many industries. John uses images that would speak to people who are tempted by the comforts of financial security. The letter challenges them to make a decision whether they will be "hot" and commit themselves to their faith, or whether they will be "cold" and abandon their faith. There is no room for middle ground. The Son of Man stands knocking at their door. If they open the door and let him in, they will share in the coming victory. If not, they will be left wretched, poor, blind, and naked.

What are the seven seals?
(Revelation 5:1–8:6)

Prophets often sealed up their visions of future events in a scroll. When John is transported to heaven, he sees a scroll with seven seals at the right hand of God. (There were actually seven scrolls, each sealed individually, one on top of another.) The question of who is worthy to open the scroll is answered quickly as we are told that only the Lamb, the crucified Jesus, is worthy to open the scroll. As each seal is broken, devastating events take place on the earth that represent the power of God over evil. This image of the destruction of evil could not help but give hope to those who were persecuted by evil forces. People would surely see the ultimate triumph of God's goodness over all that was negative.

As each successive seal is opened, the following is unleashed (See question 52):

- **First Seal**: The white horse and rider

- **Second Seal**: The red horse and rider

- **Third Seal**: The black horse and rider

- **Fourth Seal**: The pale horse and rider

- **Fifth Seal**: The cries of the martyrs for justice

- **Sixth Seal**: An earthquake—the sun turns black, the moon becomes the color of blood, the stars fall from the sky, and a gale force wind shakes the earth

- **Seventh Seal**: Silence "for what seemed half an hour" and the arrival of the angels with the seven trumpets

What are the seven trumpets? *(Revelation 8:7–11:19)*

The trumpets signal the unleashing of plagues that echo those that forced Pharaoh to release the people of Israel from slavery in Egypt (Exodus 7:8–11:10). In this case, however, the people of God need to be released from persecution by the conquering of the powers of darkness. Six of the trumpet blasts signal the release of a plague; the seventh heralds a new beginning:

- **First Trumpet:** Hail and "fire mingled with blood" rain down; one third of the earth is burned.

- **Second Trumpet:** A volcano turns one third of the sea to blood; one third of the living creatures in the sea die, and a third of the ships is destroyed.

- **Third Trumpet:** The star named *Wormwood* falls from the sky; one third of the rivers and springs are poisoned, causing the deaths of great numbers.

- **Fourth Trumpet:** A third of the sun, moon, and stars is wiped out; one third of the light fails.

- **Fifth Trumpet:** From the bottomless pit comes smoke that darkened the air; from the smoke came the hideous locust creatures. (See question 57.)

- **Sixth Trumpet:** Two hundred million troops on horses that breathed fire, smoke, and sulphur and that had tails like serpents ride out to kill a third of humankind.

- **Seventh Trumpet:** Voices in heaven proclaim: "The kingdom of this world has become the kingdom of our Lord and of his Messiah, and he will reign forever and ever."

What are the seven bowls?
(Revelation 15:1–16:21)

Another series of seven events, each initiated by an angel pouring out a bowl, completes God's judgment on the earth. Just as in the first series, the intensity of the plagues associated with each successive bowl increases. This series of events involves nature manifesting the power of God. Again, it draws to mind the plagues on Egypt and also closely mirrors the cycle of seven trumpets.

- **Bowl 1:** Terrible sores break out on those who have followed the beast.

- **Bowl 2:** The seas turn into dried-up blood, and everything in them dies.

- **Bowl 3:** The rivers and springs turn to blood.

- **Bowl 4:** The sun scorches the earth.

- **Bowl 5:** The kingdom of the beast is plunged into darkness, and yet people still do not repent (just as in the days of Noah).

- **Bowl 6:** The Euphrates River dries up to prepare a path for "the Kings of the East" to gather their armies for the battle of Armageddon.

- **Bowl 7:** A voice cries out, "It is over." The earth is ravaged by thunder, lightening, and "hundredweight" hailstones, and an earthquake.

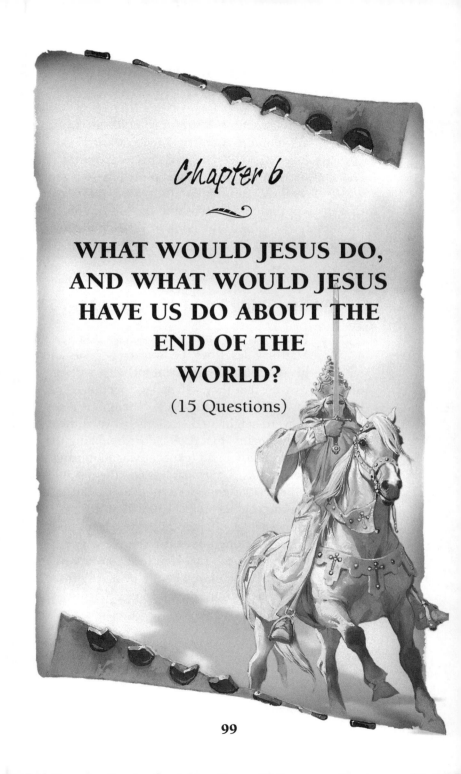

Chapter 6

WHAT WOULD JESUS DO, AND WHAT WOULD JESUS HAVE US DO ABOUT THE END OF THE WORLD?

(15 Questions)

136 Q Where does Jesus teach about the end of the world?

A Jesus' teachings about the end of the world are found in Matthew 24–25; Mark 13; and Luke 21:5-38. These teachings about the end times are most completely explored in Matthew 24–25. When we read this carefully, we begin to see that the bottom line for Jesus and the bottom line of the message of John in the Book of Revelation have much in common.

137 Q What's going on in Matthew 24–25?

A In the chapters preceding this section, Matthew describes the journey of Jesus and his disciples to Jerusalem for what will be the last Passover that they will spend together. Jerusalem was filled with all kinds of religious emotion. There were heightened tensions between the Jews and the Romans. Just days before, realizing the fevered pitch of hatred and fear that was mounting against Jesus among the Jewish leaders, the disciples had urged him not to go to Jerusalem at all. But Jesus was not one to avoid a challenge and went to Jerusalem anyway. As Chapter 24 begins, Jesus and his disciples are coming out of the Temple where they no doubt have been involved in Passover worship services. The disciples, who are primarily from rural backgrounds, admire the buildings that surround the Temple area.

138

How does Jesus get the disciples thinking about the end of the world? *(Matthew 24:2)*

As the disciples begin to talk about the cityscape rising above them, Jesus tells them that the time would come when all of the Temple buildings would be completely destroyed, leaving not one stone standing. Some interpreters have argued that Jesus foretold the future destruction of the city and the Temple in A.D. 70. Others suggest that Jesus was simply being wise about the political situation in Palestine at that time. The Jewish population actively resisted the Roman occupation. And Jesus knew, as any intelligent observer would, that the Romans would put up with this resistance only so long before they would deal with it by making an example of Israel. The Roman practice was to so utterly destroy a resisting city that not one stone was left standing on another.

139

What raises the curiosity of Jesus' disciples?

The moment the discussion turned to the destruction of the city, the disciples jumped quickly beyond the realm of politics to speculation about the end of the world, thinking that this is what Jesus was talking about. They could hardly wait to get Jesus off to their retreat on the Mount of Olives outside the city, where they would be able to talk to him in private. They assumed that if he had any direct knowledge about this end, he would tell them. Perhaps he would even be able to point out what signs to look for, so that they could be fully prepared and ready to go.

140 Q How does Jesus answer the disciples' questions? (Matthew 24:4-8)

A Jesus was a patient and caring teacher. He does not criticize their erroneous conclusions about his comment. He understands their worry and their desire for more information. Jesus begins by warning the disciples not to be misled by the many people who will attempt to deceive them. He also tells the disciples that they should not spend their time watching for signs, and should be careful to avoid misinformation and half-truths about the end.

141 Q Is Jesus aware of symbols and images used in Revelation?

A In Matthew 24:7-33, Jesus makes brief mention of a whole series of apocalyptic signs and images. He does this to demonstrate to his disciples that he "knows his stuff" when it comes to what people think about the end times. When we get to the end of this passage, however, it becomes clear that Jesus does not intend to give the disciples any specific signs or to tell them when the end will occur. Instead he says to them, "Heaven and earth will pass away, but my words will not pass away" (24:35). Jesus wants his followers to focus on his teachings about how they should live rather than on signs of the end of the world.

142 — What does Jesus mean when he says that wars and famines and earthquakes will happen but they will not signal the end?
(Matthew 24:6)

As Jesus begins to talk about events like wars, rumors of wars, natural disasters, and famines—events that are typically identified with the end of time—the disciples must have thought: *Oh boy, here it comes; he's going to tell us the signs.* Instead, Jesus repeats his warning not to be misled and says with absolute, unmistakable clarity: These things will have to happen first, but that isn't the end. So what does Jesus mean when he says this? Wars and natural disasters are everyday occurrences in this world. These realities will always be present, and we should not make the mistake of seeing them as signs, of jumping to conclusions, and of becoming fearfully obsessed with the end of the world.

143 — Does Jesus know when the end will come?
(Matthew 24:36)

So far, Jesus has told his disciples:

- Be careful about deception.

- I know what people are thinking about the end of time.

- Don't jump to conclusions about events that are part of everyday life, because "the end is not yet."

- Focus on the eternal truths of my teachings; my word will never lose its value for your life.

Then Jesus stuns his disciples by telling them that even he doesn't know when the end will come! No one except God knows when the end will come. This means that any person who says that he or she can predict the end claims an insight that even Jesus would not. Can you imagine anything that would be more presumptuous? Every time someone suggests a new scenario for the end of the world, we should remind ourselves what Jesus taught us: The timing of the end of the world is God's business!

144 Wait a minute, doesn't Jesus talk about one important sign? (*Matthew 24:15*)

Yes. Jesus warns the disciples that when they see the "Horrible Thing" (the *Contemporary English Version*) that the prophet Daniel spoke of, they should flee to the mountains. Exactly what the horrible thing will be is not clear. We know that it will defile the "holy place." Many scholars believe this refers to the presence of an idol of a foreign god. Some believe that it is another symbol for Rome, since the Romans would often erect images of the emperor on important public buildings. But whatever this horrible thing turns out to be, it will not be as important as the lesson Jesus tries to teach the disciples. Jesus lets them know that when the end has come, there will be no doubt. His followers will know. Once again he warns them: Until that time comes, do not be misled.

145 Q Does Jesus talk about the Second Coming?

A In Matthew 24:29-30, Jesus talks about the return of the Son of Man. Many of images he uses to describe this event are similar to those found in the Book of Revelation. He says that the "sun will be darkened," "the moon will not give its light," "the stars will fall from heaven," "the powers of heaven will be shaken," and the "sign of the Son of Man will appear in heaven." Once again, Jesus does not tell us what this sign will be, only that when it appears the people will see "the Son of Man coming on the clouds of heaven with power and great glory." A trumpet will sound; the Son of Man's angels will gather the elect "from the four winds, from one end of heaven to the other." From Jesus' point of view, the recognition of the Son of Man's coming will be as obvious as knowing that summer is near when the fig tree sprouts new leaves. Jesus tells the disciples that the generation that sees these signs "will not pass away until all these things have taken place."

146 Q So if we can't know for sure, what should we do?

A Be watchful. Be ready. Since the Son of Man is coming at an "unexpected hour," we need to live our lives each day as if it were the day of his coming. After telling the disciples that no one but God knows when the end will be, Jesus proceeds to teach them using three stories (Matthew 24:45–25:30). The first is the story of the faithful and unfaithful servants. In this story the master leaves and puts a servant in charge of caring for the needs of the household. The master will return unexpectedly at some time in the future. The evil slave spends the time partying, believing he will have plenty of time to do what the master expects; but he is caught off guard when the master returns. The wise servant, however, is found doing exactly what the master expected of him.

In the second story, a wedding is about to take place. But no one knows exactly when the bridegroom will arrive. The bridesmaids are instructed to watch for the groom and to prepare for his arrival. When the groom does appear, five of the brides have been wise in their waiting and watching. But five have been foolish. The wise, who are ready, go to the wedding feast; the foolish, who are not ready, are left out.
In the third story, Jesus calls upon his disciples to use the abilities, talents, and gifts they have been given for the kingdom of God. The message is clear, just as it was in the seven letters in the Book of Revelation (see Questions 111–132): Be prepared for the end by living your life as Jesus intended.

147 What does Jesus teach about the final judgment?

In Matthew 25:31-46, Jesus explains the idea of the final judgment to the disciples as a separation of the faithful from the unfaithful. Jesus does not offer the same level of detail as does the Book of Revelation. Instead, he simply says that the Son of Man will be like a shepherd separating sheep from goats. The sheep will end up on his right hand, the goats on his left.

148 So how does the Son of Man tell a sheep from a goat? (Matthew 25:31-43)

Jesus explains the basis for the separation:

> *Then the king will say to those at his right, "My father has blessed you! Come and receive the kingdom that was prepared for you before the world was created. When I was hungry, you gave me something to eat, and when I was thirsty, you gave me something to drink. When I was a stranger, you welcomed me, and when I was naked, you gave me clothes to wear. When I was sick, you took care of me, and when I was in jail, you visited me." Then the ones who pleased the Lord will ask, "When did we give you something to eat or drink? When did we welcome you as a stranger or give you clothes to wear or visit you while you were sick or in jail?" The king will answer, "Whenever you did it for any of my people, no matter how unimportant they seemed, you did it for me."'*
> (Matthew 25:34-40, CEV)

The unfaithful, of course, will fail to pass this test.

149 So what do Jesus' teachings and the Book of Revelation have in common?

The message of Jesus concerning the judgment is the same as the message of the seven letters and the Final Judgment in the Book of Revelation: "I know your works." Jesus expects us to live every day by his commandment that we love one another, rather than wasting our time worrying about when the end of the world will arrive. In terms of what Jesus teaches us, the symbols, visions, and images of the Book of Revelation are no longer the focus. Jesus wants us to center ourselves in the demands of the gospel. We are called to live faithfully, and by living a Christlike life, we will be prepared for the end of the world whenever it may come.

So tell me one more time: What is important about the Book of Revelation and Jesus' teachings about the end of the world?

 The teachings of Jesus and the Book of Revelation leave us with two powerful truths.

The first great truth is about what God will do for us. Not only will God's goodness and power ultimately and absolutely triumph over evil, but God will continuously—and eternally—take care of those who have been faithful to God. This is a message of promise; it is a message that reassures us, encourages us, and sustains us as we live in the world. It is an eternal message that gives us hope.

The second great truth concerns what we must do in response to God's wonderful promises to us: We must live out our faith. This means that what we think, what we say, and what we do should always reflect who we are in Jesus Christ. Anyone who does this has no need to worry about the end of the world. Jesus said it best: "Heaven and earth may pass away, but my words will never pass away" (24:35).

Index

Scripture		Page